D1276032

AMERICAN EVANGELICAL MISSIONARIES IN FRANCE 1945-1975

Allen V. Koop

UNIVERSITY
PRESS OF
AMERICA

LANHAM • NEW YORK • LONDON

University Press of America,® Inc.

4720 Boston Way
Lanham, MD 20706

3 Henrietta Street
London WC2E 8LU England

Library of Congress Cataloging in Publication Data

Koop, Allen V., 1944-
    American evangelical missionaries in France, 1945-
1975.

    Bibliography: p.
    Includes index.
    1. Missions—France—History—20th century.   2. France
—Church history—1945-   . I. Title.
BV2940.K66   1986   266'.023'73044   85-29431
ISBN 0-8191-5204-8 (alk. paper)
ISBN 0-8191-5205-6 (pbk. : alk. paper)

Dedication

To My Parents

Acknowledgments

Many people helped me to complete this study. Missionaries freely gave of their time to speak with me. I will not single out for special mention the dozen who were the most helpful and candid, but only as a concession to their modesty. Several missionary families extended their hospitality to me as I wandered through France. Mission agencies graciously opened their files to me. Richard Winchell and others at the Evangelical Alliance Mission were particularly helpful. Robert Evans, the Greater Europe Mission and the Conservative Baptist Foreign Mission Society shared information willingly. Colby-Sawyer College provided some travel money and arranged for Marion Stetson and Pat Hess to type the manuscript. Russell Hitt and Patricia Wetherall read portions of the manuscript. My parents offered support when the going got tough, and took their turns at the copying machine. Notes and manuscript claimed the dining table for months; my children, Jennifer and Heather, kindly coped.

Colby-Sawyer College
New London
New Hampshire
1985

Resident American Evangelical Missionaries

1955

Resident American Evangelical Missionaries

1975

Table of Contents

Chapter I   Introduction......................   1

Chapter II   New Beginnings....................   21

Chapter III   The First Wave...................   41

Chapter IV   The Search for Strategy..........   73

Chapter V   Church Planting, More or Less....   105

Chapter VI   The American Missionaries
                in French Society..............   135

Chapter VII   Conclusion.......................   163

American Evangelical Missionaries in France

1945-1975

PREFACE

This is a little story. Only a few of the events
described in these pages made news in France or
America. The number of American missionaries in
France grew continually, but they remained a small
group compared to the populations of the country to
which they journeyed and the country from which they
came. But the twentieth century has seen repeatedly a
nation's direction changed by a small, determined
group. Other movements stalled. Some were pursuers
of a lost cause, others the trustees of an idea whose
time had yet to come.

There are some aspects of American mission work
in France which are NOT covered by this study. American missionaries who participated solely in radio work
or literature publication are omitted because they had
little contact with the French people. The few
individuals who classified themselves as "independent
missionaries", although perhaps supported by American
donors, are omitted because their elusive activity
carried no affiliation with American mission agencies.
This study does not include the few American
evangelical mission boards whose interest in France
amounted only to sending funds to French evangelical
groups.

I want to tell you enough about the American
missionaries so you can understand their experience in
France, but I do not want to tell you more about them
than you wanted to know. The issues of the story are
large, even if sometimes eclipsed by the small events
of everyday living. The people in this book took on
two of the greatest problems of modern history: the
division of Christendom and the conflict of nations.

CHAPTER I

Introduction

It was going to be a hot day. Under the cover of
a dark August night in 1944 the allied invasion fleet
steamed silently to its assault positions off the
coast of Nazi-occupied southern France. Two months
earlier the first thrust of the invasion of France had
hammered ashore on the Normandy beaches. Now, Operation Anvil was poised to fling thousands of American
troops ashore between Toulon and Cannes, and then race
up the Rhone valley, pushing the retreating Germans
back to the Rhine. Robert P. Evans, the first Navy
chaplain to be assigned to a landing craft, had slept
little. As the boat rocked on the choppy sea, he
spoke quietly with his companions, studied the thick
attack plan, thumbed through his New Testament, and
awaited the explosions of gunfire which would signal
the start of the attack. Suddenly tracers and flares
lit up the sky, while bombs and shells thundered
everywhere. Eight minutes after the first wave of
soldiers hit the beaches, Evans waded in to the
Mediterranean water, felt the soil of France under his
boots, and struggled ashore with his equipment -- two
mussette bags containing Bibles and first aid
material. Quickly pushing inland with the invading
army, Evans climbed up an embankment where he first
met a French civilian. The encounter would direct the
rest of his life. Staring wide-eyed at the tanks and
trucks roaring across the sand, the swarthy peasant, a
beret on his head, was crossing himself fervently.
Evans walked up to him, mustering up his boyhood
French learned in French Cameroon where his parents
had served as Presbyterian missionaries. "Why do you
cross yourself?" Gesturing toward the beach, the
peasant replied, "Wouldn't anybody, to see this?"
Evans responded, "Oh, I thought you might be a pious
Catholic using the sign of the cross as a prayer."
Looking directly at the American who was naive enough
to offer such a comment, the Frenchman shrugged and
then spat contemptuously. "That is what I think of
all religion." And as an afterthought, the frowning
peasant said, "What has crossing oneself got to do
with religion anyway."[1]

Three days later enemy shrapnel wounded Evans
seriously. He lay unconscious for several days, and
finally awoke in a field hospital in Grasse, a French
town a few miles north of Cannes. As he recuperated

1

he talked with some of the villagers, discovering the same attitude toward religion which he had seen in the peasant on the beach. The young chaplain resolved that after the war he would return to these people as a missionary.

Evans took a position in the forefront of the postwar American evangelical missionary movement in France. Starting with a few ex-servicemen, the missionary venture grew to include a force of hundreds of missionaries and an investment of millions of dollars. By 1975 these missionaries had labored in France for a generation. Although their activities and impact in France became diverse, the goal which the evangelical missionaries set before themselves remained simple. They sought to convert French men, women, and children to belief in evangelical Christianity, and consequently to a new manner of living. The experience of these Americans in France, a story of cultural clash and theological differences, revealed the complicated relationship between national values and religious beliefs.

The American evangelical missionaries who went to France after World War II were not the first to operate in that country. After all, missionaries were responsible for bringing the infant Christian faith to southern Gaul nearly two thousand years ago.[2] But the postwar Americans, while linked by belief and heritage to the apostolic age, found more recent predecessors in missionary movements in France following the French Revolution. By that time foreign Protestants had become convinced that the tortured religious history of France had weakened French Protestantism so that it might wither without outside help.

At one time Protestantism nearly triumphed in France. In the early years of the Reformation almost thirty percent of the population embraced the new doctrines, and thousands of Protestant congregations formed throughout the country. But the military and political success of French Catholics stemmed the Protestant tide and achieved Catholic dominence. Then, a century of persecution and a continuing Huguenot emigration sapped the vitality of French Protestantism. By the beginning of the eighteenth century French Protestantism had been nearly snuffed out. Only the wild mountains of the Cévennes did Protestants conduct religious services, usually

clandestinely.[3]   Although   the   French   Revolution
renewed a measure of recognition and legal protection
to French Protestants, their depleted numbers and
weakened condition caught the eye of fellow Protestants in other European countries.   At the end of the
eighteenth century foreign missionaries appeared again
in France.   The first included a few itinerant
Moravian preachers who roamed the Cévennes, as well as
some British Methodists who went initially to the
Channel Islands and then to Normandy.[4]   A larger
influx of foreign missionaries accompanied an early
nineteenth century European Protestant revival known
as the Réveil.[5]   Starting in Geneva, the Réveil
spread to the rest of French-speaking Europe, and
assumed proportions large enough to draw French Protestantism into the larger evangelical awakening of the
first half of the nineteenth century.[6]   Foreign
missionaries from England, as well as a few Americans,
played an active role in this French revival.[7]   The
American participation in the Réveil marked the start
of a century of sporadic American missionary work in
France which formed the background for this study.
The small nineteenth century missionary venture
differed from the larger postWorld War II effort in
more than size and scope.   While the middle of the
twentieth century would offer missionaries the challenge of a modern secularized society, the Réveil participants played their roles against the backdrop of
Christendom.   The purpose of Réveil evangelism was to
find dispersed Protestants and return them to the
fold.[8]   This effort attracted the occasional support
of Bible societies and Baptist mission agencies in
America and Britain who sent evangelists and money to
aid French Bible societies.[9]   Anglo-American cooperation formed a small part of two other British-
sponsored missionary projects in nineteenth century
France.   The first led to the introduction of Plymouth
Brethren ideas to France.   Promoting the simple
separatist creed of founder J. M.   Darby, English,
Swiss and perhaps a handful of American Brethren
organized a few quiet assemblies in France.[10]   The
second of these nineteenth century missionary projects
dealt as much with the social problems of an indus-
trializing society as with the issue of personal conversion.   British organizations like the Salvation
Army and the McAll Mission (later renamed Mission
Populaire Evangélique) enrolled some Americans in
their programs of urban social work and evangelism.[11]

By the beginning of the twentieth century a challenge greater than the ills of industrialization faced
Christianity: the secularization of Christendom.
Secularization has attracted enough scholarship to
fill a library.[12] But the modern evangelical
American missionaries who might have been the most
concerned about the vanishing Christian milieu, read
little about secularization, and wrote even less.
Only a few of them attempted to grasp the causes and
dynamics of the secularizing trends which shaped and
restricted French religious life. Scholars have
broadened, bent, stretched, shrunk, twisted, and
turned the concept of secularization until it usually
obscured rather than clarified. But this pervasive
modern force which compelled a society to jettison
beliefs and practices hitherto deemed necessary to its
existence shaped the culture in which the missionaries
lived. Disagreement among its scholars about what
secularization meant discouraged missionary
comprehension of thought patterns so alien to their
Christian viewpoint.

Although most definitions of "secular" stressed
separation from anything religious, some observers of
secularization maintained that secularization itself
involved religious-like faith in secular assump-
tions.[13] Some secularization buffs contended that
secularization demanded believing in nothing, while
others said it amounted to believing in everything.[14] Another debate probed the question of
whether secularization mandated mere unbelief or absolute disbelief.[15] Some viewed the process as a
result of individual intellectual change, others as a
mass symptom of modern society.[16]

Secularization theorists pointed to a number of
causes for the secularization of Western culture, but
found little agreement on their relative importance.
Since the late Middle Ages, developments in European
philosophy and science depicted an increasingly autonomous sphere of human knowlege and activity purged of
supernatural presuppositions.[17] The Enlightenment
exalted human reason, and removed God further from
European life. Nineteenth century changes accelerated
the trends. Revolutions against political authority
called into question divine authority. New political
configurations sparked anticlerical political factions. Industrialization and urbanization moved the
masses away from nature and away from rural religious
patterns. Liberalism in thought led to scepticism.

Higher criticism undermined the authority of the Scriptures.[18] These secularizing forces affected most of Western society, but led to different types of secularization.[19] The American evangelical missionaries generally failed to probe the causes of secularization, nor did most attempt to understand how the differing forms of secularization influenced their perception of French society as well as the way in which they were perceived. Among the views of secularization, Martin Marty's tripartite discussion cataloged the issues succinctly. In England, for instance, "mere secularity" prevailed when large classes of people simply determined that God and the churches were superfluous to everyday living. In the United States, "controlled secularity" saw the retention and even expansion of Christianity, but with its practices and symbols transformed for secular purposes. While on the European continent, especially France, generations of religious and ideological conflict led to "utter secularity," devoted to the destruction and replacement of Christianity.[20] The missionaries' secular America still left plenty of room for religion. Twentieth century France, however, threatened Christianity with a harsh climate.

The turn toward pervasive secularization was taken as early as the eighteenth century. The rising French bourgeois class became increasingly indifferent to Christian precepts. While remaining Catholic, they did not want their religion to go too far. Disbelief became respectable.[21] The French Revolution intensified the contest between the Church and the growing forces of secularization. Although the next century saw moments of Catholic advance and revival, the trends went against the Church. Secular philosophies, nationalism, and socialism competed with Christianity in an increasingly bitter struggle.[22] Intense religious beliefs, practices and institutions confronted intense secular beliefs, practices and institutions.[23] Gradually the forces of organized religion lost their grip. The legal separation of church and state in France in 1905 was but one act in a long drama.[24] By the early years of the twentieth century the statisticians revealed the outcome. In Limoges, for instance, in 1899 only 2.5% of the city's children failed to be baptized; by 1914 the figure rose to over 30%.[25] Ordinations in France dropped from 1,753 in 1901 to 825 in 1913. A survey of church attendance in the department of Seine-et-Marne in 1903 placed only 2.4% of the population in

5

the category of practicing Catholics.[26]   In the
twentieth century secularization threatened to become
de-Christianization.

The twentieth century also brought three new
forms of American missionary involvement in France.
Two were intermittent and brief, the third was the
evangelical missionary movement discussed in this
book. First, relief work in France claimed the attention of some Americans between the world wars. Immediately after the First World War, American Baptists
assumed responsibility for relief projects in war-
ravaged northern France and southern Belgium.[27]
Many church buildings lay in ruins, and American money
and personnel enabled their reconstruction.[28]
Another relief project in the 1930's brought the Mennonite Central Committee to the aid of Spanish
refugees who had fled to southern France during the
Spanish Civil War.[29] Second, a few Americans
played a minor role in the introduction of pentecostal
Christianity to France in the 1930's. But this was
informal, not within the organizational structure of
mission agencies, and the exact nature and scope of
the small American involvement is difficult to ascertain.[30]

The third kind of American mission work begun in
France during the inter-war years was evangelical.
This involved only a few missionaries, but they proved
to be the forerunners of the large force of evangelical missionaries on whom this study is focused.   In
Brittany a small-scale mission combined evangelistic
aims and social work when Priscilla Johnson, a Plymouth Brethren missionary, opened an orphanage.
Although interrupted by the war, the orphanage resumed
its work in the postwar years.[31] Another missionary, Harvey L. Phelps, went to Paris in 1938, sponsored by the Brooklyn-based European Christian
Mission, later known as the Bible Christian Union.
This mission originally had been founded during World
War I for the purpose of evangelizing eastern Europe,
especially Estonia, but political conditions prompted
the mission to shift its attention to the west.   However, Phelps' work in the Paris suburb of Asnières was
cut short by the coming war.   After being held in
prison for two months and then released, Phelps made
his way across the demarcation line to unoccupied
France.   He lived in Marseille for several months,

assisting a French couple in a modest program of evangelism, and then sailed for New York in 1942.[32]

The war terminated American mission work in France, but only temporarily. Evans, Phelps, and some servicemen assigned to France determined that with the coming of peace they would return as missionaries.

The foregoing examples of missionary activity in France before 1945 were virtually unknown in America. Until the Second World War, most American Christians assumed that European churches were capable of carrying out the task of evangelism in their respective countries. The 1910 Edinburgh conference on missions, which had set the tone for mission work in the early twentieth century, did not consider Europe a mission field. Even during the war, when Americans were concerned about Europe, calls for missionary activity in Europe were rare.[33] After the war ended, however, a series of dramatic changes in the American missionary movement encouraged American evangelicals to consider France as a mission field.

The American evangelical missionaries sent to France in the postwar years took their vocation seriously. Although American citizens, although evangelical believers, they were, above all else, missionaries in thought, in values, in aspirations, and in identity. Missionary history shaped their view of the past, missionary values dictated their behavior, missionary goals drew them forward.

The missionary impulse was particularly strong in American Christianity. From the colonial period to the twentieth century, the Christian missionary movement played an important part in American culture. Even in the secular twentieth century, American missions claimed a supporting constituency which numbered in the millions. Although most did not give large amounts of their income or interest, others were more deeply involved. To a substantial minority of Americans, foreign missions were a major concern.[34]

Several significant developments shaped the course of American Protestant missions in the twentieth century. During the first part of the century the missionary movement split into camps created by the cleavage of American Protestantism into conservatives and liberals, or into fundamentalists and modernists, or into evangelicals and non-evangelicals.

The labels did not always make things clear, and sometimes the battle lines drawn between the two sides defied logical explanation.

The evangelicals distinguished themselves by their firm emphasis upon a conversion experience, often termed "being born again" or "accepting Christ." They steadfastly upheld orthodox Christian doctrines such as the authority and inspiration of Scripture, the inherent sinfulness of humanity, the literal interpretation of the virgin birth, the crucifixion as substitutionary atonement, the resurrection, the ascension, and the second coming of Christ. Evangelicals celebrated two sacraments, baptism and communion, although neither was deemed necessary for salvation. Evangelicals underscored the Reformation principle of salvation through faith alone. Those who preferred to be known as fundamentalists subscribed to these basic evangelical beliefs, but also insisted upon a strict code of social behavior, usually including taboos against smoking, drinking and often dancing and cinema. Fundamentalists tended to be separatists, refusing cooperation and even communication with Christian groups whose beliefs differed from theirs. Some took pride in "second-degree separatism", keeping apart even from fellow evangelicals who maintained relationships with more liberal Christians. Although a minority within the world of evangelical Christianity, fundamentalists often assumed a combative posture.

As far as missionary activity was concerned, evangelicals of all stripes agreed that in the early and mid-twentieth century the major American denominational mission agencies had drifted over to liberal theological positions which had reduced their missionary purpose to humanitarian aid and social work, not conversion of religious beliefs. The evangelicals, charging that the major denominational mission boards had abandoned their original evangelistic purpose, began to form their own mission agencies which were committed to conservative theological doctrines. These evangelical mission agencies could not enjoy denominational financial support, so they were obliged to develop their own support structure within the conservative churches in America. Evangelical missionaries generally saw no point in seeking cooperation or even dialogue with denominational or other liberal mission personnel. Theological differences formed a watershed in mission strategy. One spokesman summed

8

up the evangelical view of humanitarian missions: "While using Biblical words, they define missions in humanistic terms. They do not believe that it makes an eternal difference whether men accept the Lord Jesus and are baptized in His name. They do not believe that in the Bible we have the authoritative, infallible Word of God."[35] As important as social work might be, evangelicals emphasized that it was "no substitute for the redemption of sinful, unbelieving men."[36] Personal conversion was the goal of their mission work.

The American evangelical missionary venture in France was influenced by developments in the world-wide missionary movement following World War II. At first, missionary leaders plunged into pessimism and gloom when shocking political changes terminated mission work in China and curtailed missionary activity in the former colonial world from which the West was retreating. But then a surprising reversal opened the greatest expansion in the history of missions.[37]

The newly independent nations of the third world attracted a renewed and diversified missionary penetration. Contrary to the popular assumption that Christianity was everywhere on the decline, it made great gains, mainly in the third world.

In spite of the upheavals of the twentieth century, and in spite of the progressive secularization and even de-Christianization of Western culture, Christianity was a more potent force worldwide in mid-century than it had been in 1914.[38] Christianity was taking root in the cultures of more peoples than at any time in history. Examples of the phenomenal growth were numerous: the church in Korea grew more between 1953 and 1960 than it had in the previous sixty years; the church in sub-Saharan Africa increased from thirty million to ninety-seven million; at least 50,000 Indonesian Moslems became Christians.[39]

Missionaries played a major role in this recent worldwide expansion of Christianity, and North American missionary agencies had grown to dominate the worldwide missionary force. Furthermore, by the 1970's the complexion of the North American missionary movement had changed to reflect the growth of evangelical power in American religion. At first dismissed as superficial postwar revivalism, the evangelical renaissance which began in the 1950's went much deeper and wider than early sceptical observers indicated, and by the 1970's nearly a majority of Americans were associated by pollsters with evangelical or "born again" religious experiences.[40] Missionary statistics reflected the burgeoning evangelical movement in the United States. In 1953, conservative evangelical missions fielded 9,216 career missionaries, while the liberal mainline denomination missions claimed 10,416. By 1973 the number of mainline Protestant missionaires had slipped to 6,921, while those of the conservative evangelical missions had climbed to 25,140.[41]

However, in spite of the dramatic growth of missionary activity and the expansion of Christianity into new areas, a look at the big picture rendered a mixed verdict. The Christian optimists added up the growing numbers of missionaries, converts, churches, and church members. The pessimists looked at other numbers and concluded that the explosive population growth in the third world served to shrink the Christian per cent of the world each day.[42]

All of this had a significant impact upon the missionaries in France because of their strong relationship with the worldwide community of evangelical missionaries. No matter how absorbed they became in their narrow everyday tasks, the missionaries in France walked in the ranks of two major historical movements: the expansion of American influence in the postwar world and the surge of evangelical missions. The missionaries must be counted among the large number of Americans who worked in postwar France in business, military, or cultural capacities, but they had little to do with the other Americans, and felt no particular relationship to them. The missionaries took their cues from other missionaries around the world, not from the Americans in Paris. The French, however, viewed them as part of the new American invasion. This saddled the missionary enterprise in France with a continuing problem of confused identity and purpose.

Who were these missionaries? The people encountered in this study formed a generally homogenous group. The midwest and Pennsylvania supplied the majority of the American missionary force in France. Most missionaries were born into large families (often four children or more) who considered themselves to be in the lower middle class. While their work in France normally took them to urban areas, most missionaries had been raised in a rural or small-town environment. Although a few of the missionaries had been converted as adults, most professed a childhood or early adolescence conversion experience, and many claimed to have been called to the life of a missionary as teenagers. Their home church affiliation was usually with an independent Baptist or evangelical church of small or medium size. Only a very few of the missionaries to nominally Catholic France had made their own conversion from a Catholic religious background in America.

The educational experience of the missionaries revealed a basic uniformity in spite of the large number of institutions represented. Most missionaries graduted from Bible institutes or Bible colleges, while some held degrees from liberal arts colleges and theological seminaries. Wheaton College (Illinois), Columbia Bible College, Bob Jones University, and Moody Bible Institute counted the most graduates among the missionary force in France. The number of missionaries with advanced degrees rose in the 1960's, as several used furlough time for additional education. In the 1970's a few began doctoral studies at European universities. Most missionaries went to France as married couples, and husbands and wives shared similar economic, geographic, educational and religious backgrounds. It was common for missionaries to head for France as soon as they had completed their schooling, but there were some who had held previous employment. Of these, most had been pastors or missionaries in other countries, while those who had been employed secularly held positons ranging from college teacher to egg picker in a hen house.

Aside from their general education, most missionaries received little specific preparation for their work in France. Only a few possessed any experience with the French language, and those who attempted to read about French culture and history usually confined their investigations to sources like the National Geographic magazine, encyclopedias, and mission agency magazines. The most influential single source of information was missionary Robert Evans' book, Let Europe Hear, published in 1963.[43] Most missionaries confessed that the traditional methods of missionary support and training created little time or incentive for adequate preparation. The evangelical mission agencies required prospective missionaries to raise their own financial support by arranging for friends, relatives, or churches to pledge a certain amount of money toward their support. When enough people made a commitment sufficient to cover the cost of round trip transporation and support in France, the missionary was able to leave. Raising this money could take a long time, usually twelve to thirty-six months. Therefore, once someone decided to go to France as a missionary, he or she usually plunged immediately into the task of "deputation," or raising support. In the course of hectic travel from city to city and church to church, there was little time to study or read.

The culmination of the pre-departure preparation took the form of a candidate school or orientation session held by the sending mission. But these exercises focused upon general mission policies rather than specific details of the country to which the missionary was going. For many missionaries the differences between mission fields were of little consequence. At least one third of the missionaries in France had originally planned to serve in third world countries, but changed to France at the last minute without a basic change of purpose. Mission policies sustained this attitude. An early pamphlet of one large American mission referred to its "mission stations" in France, just as it referred to the same in Africa or Asia.[44] So, while most missionaries possessed a solid background in theology and even in mission theory, they gained little specific training for France. Consequently the missionaries, often young and inexperienced, arrived with visionary goals of evangelizing France, only to find how poorly prepared they were for living in a new culture where even ordinary activities like taking the metro to language study could be trying experiences.

Although the missionaries' educational, social, and economic background shaped their work in France, nothing was more important than their basic religious beliefs. The evangelical missionary's world view was determined by a conviction that the Bible was true and that anything opposed to the Bible was false. Their avowed commitment to Biblical instruction led many missionaries to contend that the most important element in bringing success to their work was the intensity of their own religious life. One of the most successful and culturally sensitive missionaries, thoroughly trained in theology, stressed that he would have been more productive if he had known the Bible better. Missionary correspondence and furlough activity revealed the uniform conviction that a success in France could occur only if supported by extensive prayer in America.

The firmly held belief in the intervention of God in human lives had a corollary in the missionaries' belief in the reality of the other side of the supernatural: Satan and the realm of spiritual evil. In letter after letter and article after article the missionaries ascribed to Satan the commonly seen practices of the occult in France. Although specific occult manifestations (demon possession, rattling objects in houses, etc.) were infrequently reported, on several occasions the missionaries claimed to have had direct confrontation with the forces of evil. A few claimed to have been instrumental in exorcisms. More common were recurrent references to the constant yet unspecified Satanic influence which they said hindered the progress of missionary work in France. In official annual reports as well as in personal letters and newsletters, missionaries frequently attributed the failure of specific projects as well as the frustrating lack of general progress to the power of Satanic opposition to the gospel in France: "the devil is doing his best to discourage us in the work."[45] Belief in the reality of supernatural opposition was strengthened in the minds of many by the personal tragedies which befell missionary families: illness, accidents, and the death of a number of missionary children. The literature of the American evangelical missionary movement in postwar France provides abundant evidence that the missionaries believed their work to be part of a supernatural spiritual struggle between the forces of Satan and those of God.

The story told on these pages takes place against the backdrop of two larger issues of the twentieth century. The first concerns the place of Christianity in modern Europe, the continent which for nearly two thousand years was the center of Christendom. The majority opinion has ruled that Christian Europe has seen its day. Secularists legitimize and applaud this development of history, regarding the pockets of religiosity in Europe as anachronistic remnants of an age rapidly receding into the past. Even within Christianity a growing number of observers, while refusing to accept the legitimacy of secularization, nonetheless concede that Europe has had its chance with Christianity, and that the gospel has moved on to the masses of Africa, Asia, and Latin America. European Christians in the twentieth century form a remnant, albeit a faithful one, digging in for a protracted holding action in a hostile or, perhaps worse, indifferent society. Then there are a few analysts with a view more cyclical than linear who see in twentieth century Europe a neo-paganism akin to that which yielded to the first Christian missionaries more than seventeen hundred years ago.

The second theme concerns the conflict between cultural and theological standards, the relationship between relative and absolute values. The American evangelical missionary movement in France grew dramatically in personnel and in financial investment. But their efforts were often unavailing, and the success-oriented Americans, convinced of the eternal value of their redemptive message, came to grips with only limited success and frequent failure. Problems of cultural identity plagued the missionaries torn between American and French cultures. Particularly acute was the tension stemming from the differences between French culture and the subculture of American evangelical Christianity. The missionaries tended to view cultural issues in theological terms. Cultural adaptation became a theological dilemma.

As other foreigners in France, the American missionaries experience varying degrees of culture shock as they sought to adapt to their new environment. But they attempted to change French society at the same time they attempted to conform to it. The problems they faced doing both opened an intense debate within missionary circles. Were they and their message cast too rigidly in an American mold ever to win acceptance in France? Or were the French too proud and sensitive about their culture to give approval to the Americans, no matter how earnest and successful they were in adapting to French customs? What was the relationship between religious belief and cultural behavior, both French and American?

The work of American evangelical missionaries in France has been virtually ignored by secular histories of the postwar era, and all but ignored by religious scholarship. Secular historians writing for a secular age tend to ignore religious questions. Religious studies of postwar France concentrate upon the

14

Catholic or Reformed churches, and usually omit reference to the persistent presence of the American missionaries. The French scholar Emile Leonard notes contributions made by Americans to French Protestantism in the areas of piety and doctrine, but in his exhaustive study of modern Protestantism he fails to discuss the American missionary work in postwar France.[46] The American missionary activity is acknowledged in Raoul Stephan's Histoire du Protestantisme Francaise, but only when he makes passing references to the European Bible Institute, the oldest and largest of the institutions created by the missionaries.[47]

Even the literature of Christian missions makes little of missionary work in France. Typcially, a general history of missions by Stephen Neill devotes only one page to the state of Christianity in Europe, and makes no mention of American missionary personnel in France.[48] The literature of evangelical missions in particular, preoccupied with accomplishments in Asia, Africa, and Latin America, postponed including the growing American missionary work in Europe. The standard evangelical surveys of missions neglected the Americans in France until the mid-1960's, almost twenty years after the beginning of the postwar missionary activity.[49] This underscores the strange and significant isolation of the missionary forces within French society. Their small impact, largely unnoticed by the secular world, was due not only to the resistance of French culture to their message, but also to the attitudes and policies of the missionaries which led them to separate themselves from the society which they were trying to convert.

CHAPTER I NOTES

[1]Interview with Robert Evans, March 6, 1973; Robert P. Evans, Let Europe Hear (Chicago: Moody Press, 1963), pp. 107-108.

[2]Kenneth Scott Latourette, A History of the Expansion of Christianity, Vol. I, The First Five Centuries, (Grand Rapids: Zondervan Publishing House, 1970), p. 98.

[3]Reuben Saillens, The Soul of France (London: Morgan and Scott, Ltd., 1927), pp. 75-99; Frank Orna-Ornstein, France: Forgotten Mission Field (Foxton, England: Burlington Press, 1971), pp. 81, 98.

[4]Orna-Ornstein, p. 118; World Council of Churches, Ecumenical Studies: Evangelism in France (Geneva: Secretariat for Evangelism, World Council of Churches, December, 1951), pp. 6, 7.

[5]World Council of Churches, pp. 7, 8. See also Adrian Dansette, Religious History of Modern France (New York: Herder and Herder, 1961), II, 25; Francis R. Guittee, Historie de l'Eglise de France (12 vols., Paris: Bureau de l'administration de l'histoire de l'Eglise de France, 1965), XII, pp. 176-177; Henry H. Walsh, The Concordat of 1801 (New York: Columbia University Press, 1933), p. 57.

[6]Kenneth Scott Latourette, Christianity in a Revolutionary Age, Vol. II: The Nineteenth Century in Europe (New York: Harper Brothers, 1959), p. 227; Samuel Mours, Un siècle d'évangélisation en France 1815-1914 (2 vols., Paris: Librairie Protestante, 1963), I, 14, 253-254; Paul Conord, Protestantisme Francais d'aujourd'hui (Paris: A. Coueslant, 1959), 69 ff.

[7]Latourette, Christianity in a Revolutionary Age, Vol. II, p. 227; Jacques Blocher, "The Influence of Foreign Missionaries in France," a report to the semi-annual conference of the Evangelical Alliance Mission, (TEAM) Novembr, 1960, p. 6; Emile Leonard, Le Protestante Francaise (Paris: Presses Universitaires de France, 1964); Robert P. Evans, "The Contribution of Foreigners to the French Protestant Reveil 1815-1850" (unpublished Ph. D. dissertation, University of Manchester, 1971), pp. 371-486; Daniel Robert, Les

Eglises Reformées en France (Paris: Presses Universitaires de France, 1961), pp. 349, 353-357, 370.

[8]World Council of Churches, pp. 6, 7.

[9]Evans, "Contribution . . .," pp. 373-481.

[10]Latourette, Christianity in a Revolutionary Age, Vol. II, p. 133; Evans, "Contribution . . .," pp. 229-238; Orna-Ornstein, p. 119; Maurice Colinon, Le Phénomene des sectes au XXe siècle (Paris: Librairie Arthème Fayard, 1959), pp. 52-54.

[11]Georges Velten, Mission in Industrial France (London: SCM Press, 1968); Latourette, Christianity in a Revolutionary Age, pp. 8, 9; Orna-Ornstein, pp. 119-120.

[12]A few of many: David Martin, A General Theory of Secularization (New York: Harper & Row, 1978); Martin Marty, The Modern Schism (New York: Harper & Row, 1969); Varieties of Unbelief (New York: Holt, Rinehart and Winston, 1964); The New Shape of American Religion (New York: Harper & Row, 1958); The Public Church (New York: Crossroad, 1981); Roger Mehl, The Sociology of Protestantism (Philadelphia: Westminster Press, 1970); Traite de sociologie du protestantisme (Neuchatel: Delachaux & Niestle, 1965); P. P. Pin-Carrier, Essais de sociologie religieuse (Paris: Spes, 1967); Seward Salisbury, Religion in American Culture (Homewood, Illinois: Dorsey, 1964); F. Boulard, An Introduction to Religious Sociology (London: Darton, Longman and Todd, 1960); Susan Budd, Sociologists and Religion (London: Collier-Macmillan, 1973); Herbert Butterfield, Christianity in European History (London: Collins, 1952); Owen Chadwick, The Secularization of the European Mind in the Nineteenth Century (Cambridge: Cambridge Press, 1975); D. G. Charlton, Secular Religions in France 1815-1870 (London: Oxford University Press, 1963); Christopher Dawson, Progress and Religion (Garden City: Image, 1960).

[13]Marty, The Modern Schism, p. 1; Varieties of Unbelief, p. 60.

[14]Marty, Varieties of Unbelief, p. 61.

[15]Marty, Varieties of Unbelief, p. 27.

[16]Mehl, pp. 60-62.

[17]B. Groethuysen, "Secularism," Encyclopedia of Social Sciences, ed. Edwin Seligman (New York: Macmillan, 1948), p. 631.

[18]Chadwick, pp. 21, 86, 94, 107, 219-220.

[19]Martin, p. 35.

[20]Marty, The Modern Schism, pp. 18, 59, 95.

[21]B. Groethuysen, Origines de l'Espirit en France (L'Eglise et la Bougeoisie) (Paris: Librairie Gallimard, 1927), pp. 15, 24, 32.

[22]Charlton, D. G., Secular Religions in France 1815-1870 (London: Oxford University Press, 1963).

[23]Martin, p. 7.

[24]A. Coutrot and F. Dreyfus, Les Forces religieuses dan la societe Francaise (Paris: Librairie Armand Colin, 1965).

[25]Dansette, Vol. II, p. 417.

[26]John McManners, Church and State in France, 1870-1914 (London: SPCK, 1972), p. 169.

[27]Olive Dale, "L'Evangélisation en Belgique Pendant l'entre-deux-guerres" (unpublished thesis, Faculté Libre de Théologie Evangélique, Vaux-sur-Seine, 1972), p. 10.

[28]Missions, American Baptist Foreign Mission Society, September, 1919, pp. 704, 737; Louise S. Houghton, Handbook of French and Belgian Protestantism (New York: Federal Council, Churches of Christ, 1919), pp. 183-184.

[29]John D. Unruh, In the Name of Christ (Scottsdale, Pennsylvania: Herald Press, 1952), pp. 45-47.

[30]George Stotts, "The History of the Modern Pentecostal Movement in France," (unpublished Ph. D.

dissertation, Texas Tech University, 1973); Blocher p. 11; Orna-Ornstein, p. 120.

[31]Letter from Priscilla Johnson to the author, July, 1973.

[32]Harvey Phelps, Gold's Deliverance From Nazi Hands (Brooklyn: European Christian Mission, 1944).

[33]Adolph Kellar, Christian Europe Today (New York: Harper Brothers, 1942), p. 228.

[34]Kenneth Scott Latourette, Missions and the American Mind (Indianapolis: National Foundation Press, 1949), pp. 3, 5, 31, 32; Elton Trueblood, The Validity of the Christian Mission (New York: Harper & Row, 1972), pp. ix, 10; "The New Missionary," Time, December 27, 1982, pp. 50-56.

[35]Donald McGavran (ed.), The Eye of the Storm (Waco, Texas: Word Books, 1972), p. 81.

[36]Donald McGavran (ed.), The Eye of the Storm, p. 179. See also Harold Lindsell, A Christian Philosophy of Missions (Wheaton, Illinois: Van Kampen Press, 1949).

[37]Kane, A Global View of Christian Missions (Grand Rapids: Baker Book House, 1971), p. 219; Harlan Cleveland, Gerald Mangone, John Adams, The Overseas Americans (New York: Arno Press, 1980), p. 82.

[38]Latourette, Christianity in a Revolutionary Age, Vol. 5, p. 526.

[39]Ralph D. Winter, The Twenty-five Unbeliev-able Years (Pasadena: William Carey Library, 1970), pp. 41, 61.

[40]William McLoughlin and Robert Bellah, eds., Religion in America (Boston: Beacon Press, 1968), p. X; Time, December 21, 1977, pp. 52-58; Newsweek, May 6, 1974, p. 86; Christianity Today, December 21, 1979, pp. 12-14.

[41]Robert T. Cooke, "The Uneven Growth of Con-servative Evangelical Missions," International Bulle-tin of Missionary Research, Vol. 6, No. 3, July, 1982, p. 120. See also Mission Handbook: North American

Protestant Ministries Overseas, 10th and 12th ed. (Monrovia, California: Missions Advanced Research and Communication Center, 1973 and 1979), p. 94 (10th ed.) and p. 120 (12th ed.); Time, December 27, 1982, p. 54. A 1972 New York Times study revealed losses of up to 30% in some mainline denomination missions, losses of nearly 10% in Catholic missions, but continued increases in evangelical missions., New York Times, March 12, 1972, p. E8.

[42]Marty, Varieties of Unbelief, p. 43.

[43]Robert P. Evans, Let Europe Hear (Chicago: Moody Press, 1963).

[44]"Latin Lands of Lingering Legends and Lasting Traditions," The Evangelical Alliance Mission (TEAM), Wheaton, Illilnois, early 1950's.

[45]Letter, R. Johnston to David Johnson, February, 1955, TEAM.

[46]Emile Leonard, Le Protestante Francaise (Paris: Presses Universitaires de France, 1953); Histoire Générale du Protestantisme (Paris: Presses Universitaires de France, 1964). R. Mandrou, et. al., Histoire des Protestants en France (Toulouse: E. Privat, 1977), omits reference to the American missionaries.

[47]Raoul Stephan, Histoire du Protestantisme Francaise (Paris: Librairee Arthemè Fayard, 1961), pp. 326, 336.

[48]Stephen Neill, A History of Christian Missions (Harmondsworth, Middlesex: Penguin, 1964).

[49]Robert P. Evans, Let Europe Hear, p. 31; Robert H. Glover, The Progress of World Wide Missions (New York: Harper Brothers, 1960); J. Herbert Kane, A Global View of Christian Missions (Grand Rapids: Baker Book House, 1971).

CHAPTER II

NEW BEGINNINGS

Life was an ordeal in postwar France. Although peace and victory helped eclipse the tragedy and shame of the German conquest, the end of the war also brought a sobering awareness of the extent of the physical and emotional damage suffered by the French people. French cities and villages had been bombed to rubble first by foe, and then by friend. The war-torn transportation network made travel a difficult chore. Shops and businesses lay demolished. Homes were dismembered or destroyed. Countless families and individuals suffered the hardship of living in ruins. The nation's economy languished in disarray, depleted by the demands of the German war machine and disrupted by the recent combat on French soil.

The emotional damage suffered by society and individuals, though less visible, was perhaps more serious. In many cases family life had disintegrated. Fathers and husbands had been killed, imprisoned, or deported. Women and children, even if spared the physical danger of combat zones, had borne the burdens and temptations of separation and anxiety. The Nazi occupation, the Vichy regime, and the resistance movements had combined to confront the French with bewildering options and severe ethical trials. Although the wounds healed slowly, the scars remained.

The end of the war revealed the weakness of French Christianity. Church buildings had been destroyed, clergy and laymen killed, and congregations dispersed. But the loss of personnel and buildings was not the main problem. The war and occupation had opened the eyes of a concerned minority within the French churches to the pervasive de-Christianization of French society. H. Godin's La France: Pays de Mission, published during the war, demonstrated the extent to which the masses of France had deserted the Roman Catholic church.[1] Cardinal Souhard's pastoral letter, circulated at the end of the war, dealt soberly with the challenge of a declining church.[2] The World Council of Churches published conclusions of convincing case studies which confirmed the notion of total de-Christianization in various geographical areas and social classes of modern France.[3] Subsequent studies marshalled more documentation to contend

that urban France was "basically pagan."[4]   American
church historians Kenneth S. Latourette and Martin
Marty later agreed.[5]   French religious sociologists
moved into rural France, and while noting significant
regional variation, forced the conclusion that "a complete picture of religious vitality in France would
show that at least four-fifths of the population have
no contact whatsoever with the Christian Church, and
live in total ignorance of the Gospel."[6]   Concerned
Catholic voices were joined by conservative Protestant
leaders like Bordeaux social scientist Jacques Ellul.
The French, he claimed, had abandoned Christianity for
political and materialistic substitutes.   "Christian
concerns became simply irrelevant, and Christian words
(piety, salvation, grace, redemption) awaken no echo
in the modern French mind."[7]   Most important, Ellul
stressed,

> all that is left of Christianity is morality,
> a bourgeois morality with which everyone is
> familiar, and a few conventional ideas (the
> clergy have a role to play in society; the
> cathedrals are an attractive element of the
> civic scene).   Post-Christian society, there-
> fore, is not simply a society which followed
> upon Christendom.   It is a society which is no
> longer Christian, a society that has had the
> experience of Christianity, is the heir of the
> Christian past, and believes it has full know-
> ledge of the Christian religion because it
> retains vague memories of it and sees remnants
> of it all around.   Nothing new, surprising, or
> unexpected, above all nothing relevant to
> modern life can come from Christianity; the
> church and the faith are simply vestiges from
> the past.[8]

This was the society which challenged the American
evangelical missionaries.   When they arrived in France
they concurred readily with the conclusions of Protestant and Catholic leaders concerned about the
de-Christianization of France.   But the American missionaries claimed that the French churches themselves
needed evangelization.   As far as Catholicism was
concerned, the evangelicals simply regarded all Catholics as lost souls who needed to be converted in order
to be saved.   They made little or no attempt to
accomodate or even understand the various factions of
belief and practice within French Catholicism.   This
crippled their efforts.   In spite of a series of

twentieth-century blows - separation of church and state, the impact of two world wars and the depression, extensive de-Christianization - the Roman Catholic church remained a vital force in France.[9] As many as 85% of the French people continued to identify themselves as Catholics, at least through baptism, and for most people in France Christianity and religion meant Catholicism.[10] There were, of course, areas of strength and weakness. Only between 10% and 20% denoted themselves as continual or practicing believers, the rest falling into periodical, occasional, or non-practicing categories.[11] The church distinguished regional differences including pagan areas (the Paris region, Acquitane basin, Mediterranean coast), Christian areas (rural Vendée, Alsace, Basses Pyrenees), and areas in between where belief persevered while practice diminished.[12] Peasant communities, especially in the South, still combined Catholic and pagan tradition, while sophisticated urbanites would embrace the modernizing trends of Vatican II.[13] The number of priests declined, but millions of pilgrims continued to visit Lourdes and other shrines.[14] Even in de-Christianized France the Catholic church influenced society and dominated religious life. The missionaries never came to grips with this.

They did not do much better with the French Protestants. There were relatively few Protestants in France. Postwar surveys placed their number between 700,000 and 1,500,000, with most settling on a figure of 800,000 or approximately 2% of the population. Of these about 450,000 belonged to the Reformed Church, 310,000 were Lutherans (mainly in Alsace), with the remainder divided among the smaller denominations like the Baptists, Assemblies of God, Mennonites, Free Churches, and the Brethren. Weekly Protestant church attendance in France ran as low as 180,000.[15] Protestant strength in France concentrated in a few regions: Alsace-Lorraine, the Cévennes and Bas Languedoc area, the lower Rhone valley, the Charente and Paris.[16] The rest lay scattered across the country. Closely identified with the commercial upper bourgeoisie, the Protestant community in France wielded influence far greater than its small size indicated.[17] Preoccupied with its martyred past (the Reformed Church maintained nine museums), Protestantism cut a low profile in modern France.[18] Of the approximately 38,000 towns in France, Protestant directories published throughout the postwar period listed only slightly more than 2,600 communities in which they noted a Protestant service. Of these only about 1,000 maintained a resident pastor or an established Protestant church.[19] Therefore, evangelicals often cited the existence of 36,000 towns without organized Protestant activity as a primary reason for the missionary work in France. Evangelical missionaries, Protestants themselves, were shocked and then discouraged to find so little Protestantism in this nominally Christian country with its Huguenot heritage. Their efforts to win converts to evangelical Protestantism suffered because most Frenchmen had no contact with Protestantism and knew little about it.

The missionaries were disturbed more by the theology of the French Protestants than by their small numbers. Except for a small conservative minority, French Protestant leaders traditionally maintained liberal theological principles which were anathema to evangelicals, extending occasionally to twentieth-century novelties like Christian atheism, and Marxist Christianity.[20] In some departments, Reformed parishioners consistently voted for communists.[21] Even the few examples of growth in this declining Protestant community, most notable the Taize community,[22] marched under the liberal ecumenical banner.[22] The missionaries kept their distance from these people. Even though the Catholics considered regions of France as mission fields, most French Protestants resented the evangelical implication that France was a mission field, and they were amazed to find missionaries among them.[23]

However, within French Protestantism were the French evangelicals, and with these the Americans felt doctrinal compatibility. But if Protestant numbers were small, evangelical numbers were tiny. Jacques Blocher, a leader in French evangelical circles, referred to them as a minority within a minority.[24] The number of evangelicals in postwar France was even more difficult to derive than that of Protestants in general. Blocher estimated that there were 20,000 to 30,000 outside the Reformed and Lutheran churches with perhaps an equal number within these French denominations. Coordinators for the Billy Graham Crusades in Paris made reference to 20,000 Parisian evangelicals out of a total French evangelical community of 50,000 or 60,000. Later estimates made by American missionaries and French evangelicals arrived at a figures of 79,000. Marcel Tabailloux, editor of the Annuaire Evangélique, a directory of evangelical churches in France, suggested that evangelicals numbered as many as 100,000 persons. But this small section of French society was never known for its unity. Divided unevenly into no fewer than thirty-seven groups, the French evangelical community was too fragmented to speak with one voice. In addition to the evangelicals in the Reformed church the largest groups of French evangelicals included the Assemblies of God, the Union of Independent Evangelical Reformed Churches (a conservative offshoot of the Reformed Church), and the Baptists. Since the majority of American missionaries in France came from Baptist churches, it was with this last group that they formed the most extensive relationship. However, fragmentation was a problem here, for the Baptists in France, few as they were, had splintered themselves into three groups: the Federation of Baptist Churches in France (the largest and most theologically diverse), the Association of Evangelical Baptist Churches (very fundamentalist), and the independent Baptists (whose Tabernacle Baptist Church was often referred to as the foremost evangelical church in Paris).[25] Misunderstandings, theological differences, and even petty squabbling kept Baptists in France, French and American, from close cooperation.

The French evangelical Christians added a new twist to the missionary movement in France. It was difficult enough to adapt missionary methods to a de-Christianized society. Missionaries traditionally sought to introduce Christianity to pagan societies. Re-introduction to a secularized or even de-Christianized society brought a host of new problems. Paradoxically, one of these stemmed from de-Christianization which although pervasive was incomplete. The small evangelical church in France still clung to life, and rather than having been founded by the missionaries (like indigenous churches in most mission fields), it antedated their arrival by centuries.

The missionaries and the French evangelicals did not always agree about a crucial question: the role of the church in society. Aggressively evangelistic, the missionaries lamented the more passive role assumed by the French evangelicals. For generations French evangelicals assumed as their primary mission the preservation of the gospel rather than the propagation of the faith. Therefore, they emphasized not numbers, but the integrity of their religious heritage which they traced to the Reformation, the Waldensians, and even to apostolic Christianity.[26]

Because they considered the Reformed seminaries in Paris and Montpellier too liberal in theological orientation, the French evangelicals relied upon two small schools to train the personnel necessary for the maintenance of their tradition. The Nogent Bible Institute was founded by Reuben Salliens in 1921 in the Paris suburb of Nogent-sur-Marne. It depended primarily upon part-time and visiting faculty to train pastors and teachers. The second school was a seminary established in Aix-en-Provence just before World War II by pastors of the dissident Independent Evangelical Reformed Church. After the war it was kept alive chiefly because of heavy subsidies from the United States raised by Donald G. Barnhouse, a well known radio preacher and pastor of Philadelphia's Tenth Presbyterian Church. Following a decade of struggling existence, the school succumbed to internal problems and dwindling enrollment. Not until the mid-1970's was there a serious attempt to revive it.

Although French evangelicalism in many ways bore a foreign stamp because of the assistance provided by foreigners throughout its history, the relationship between the French evangelicals and the postwar American missionaries presented problems. The Americans at times found the French insular in outlook, bereft of vision, and prone to bickering. The French occasionally proved unreceptive to criticism or even aid from the recent arrivals from the New World. It took a long time for the American missionaries and the French evangelicals to begin to understand each other. The Americans were slow to realize that their work in a de-Christianized France with an ancient church initiated a novel and unique form of missionary work, and often they were mystified by the French evangelicals' negative reaction to their activity.

The American evangelical missionaries in postwar France fell into three groups. First, but not foremost, were the itinerant evangelists. Second came those who sought to found evangelical institutions. Third, and eventually the largest group, were those who focused their efforts on starting new evangelical churches.

It was only several months after the end of the second World War when American missionaries began to arrive in France. Many of these early "missionaries" were little more than itinerant evangelists who were conducting whirlwind speaking tours of European cities. Making no effort to devise a strategy or method for working in France, they merely attempted to repeat programs which had been successful in the United States. Usually their activity took the form of an evangelistic team which made one or two appearances in a city and then moved on. Sometimes the "mission" amounted to little more than an airport meeting between some French churchmen and the globe-trotting leader of an American organization who came bearing gifts. Many of these groups, discouraged by the lack of response, abandoned further attempts to work in France. But some made an attempt to overcome their early blunders and to conform their approach to French culture.

The first major American missionary movement in post-war France was also the flashiest. In the late 1940's evangelistic teams from an organization known as Youth For Christ conducted rallies in a large number of French cities, and drew crowds larger than any mission before or since. During World War II Youth For Christ earned a reputation for bold evangelism through mass meetings across the United States and Canada. The leaders of Youth For Christ had built their programs around a combination of lighting, sound, and dress, occasionally referred to as "evangelical vaudeville."[27] The combination of patriotism, religion, and hoopla attracted thousands of youngsters, culminating in the Memorial Day 1945 rally which saw over 70,000 in Chicago's Soldier Field.[28] Intending to export its rallies overseas, the oranization changes its official title to Youth for Christ, International, and leader Torrey M. Johnson proclaimed its purpose to be the "evangelization of the world."[29] Energy and lofty aspirations abounded.

The Youth For Christ work in France came under the direction of former naval chaplain Robert Evans. Born in Baltimore, Evans grew up in French West Africa where his parents were missionaries, but completed his education in the United States at Wheaton College and

Eastern Baptist Theological Seminary. His first step was to press his former college friend Billy Graham, then the leading itinerant evangelist for Youth For Christ, to extend his 1946 agenda to France. Then, in April 1947, Evans arrived in Paris to discover that a small Youth For Christ program already had been initiated by some American soldiers from the American garrison in the Paris area. Meetings for youth convened on a regular basis at the American church on the Quai d'Orsay.

Evans not only assumed the direct supervision of the Youth For Christ movement in France, but he also devoted time to expand the work throughout Europe. In the late 1940's American evangelicals were caught up in feverish planning for world evangelism. Some of this was due to the climate of the cold war. The political and military victories of communist forces in Eastern Europe and China alarmed many American evangelicals. They were fearful that additional countries might soon close their doors to missionaries. In an emergency atmosphere, many missionary enthusiasts sought to use American affluence and energy in a series of intense and far-flung evangelistic enterprises. Some of these were ill-conceived and superficial. But others were diligent attempts to marshall evangelical resources for a sustained missionary effort. Among the more significant and influential meetings of this era was the first World Congress on Evangelism which convened in August 1948 at Beatenberg, Switzerland. Evans was one of the principal organizers of this congress, and soon became recognized as one of the most active American evangelicals in Europe. Before long he was able to set up Youth for Christ committees in European countries from France to Poland.

In France the Youth For Christ personnel based their work upon youth rallies. Often the crowds were large. In the years immediately after the war most religious groups in France found it relatively easy to draw a crowd.[30] The drabness of the first years of peace and the scarcity of public entertainment prompted an unusual willingness of the French to attend public meetings, even religious ones. At the height of its postwar popularity, Youth For Christ attracted 4,000 or 5,000 French youth to each rally. Sometimes the figure ran as high as 10,000.[31] But the work met with something less than universal acclaim. The evangelistic enterprise was criticized as being frothy, superficial, sensational, and unstable.[32] The organization failed to coordinate a plan to sustain the results of the one-night rallies. Although some of the Youth For Christ converts from the late 1940's became sincere evangelicals, (a few became pastors) most drifted away.

Evans became convinced that youth rallies offered a relatively fruitless way to accomplish the evangelization of France. In 1949 he resigned from Youth For Christ in order to investigate more productive forms of missionary work. By this time the Youth For Christ work in France had begun to dwindle. Perhaps the novelty had vanished, perhaps the slightly improved pattern for daily living in France had diverted attention of the youth, but for some reason the crowds became thinner and the response less encouraging. Dissension and personal problems within the leadership of the organization undermined the program.

By 1950 Youth For Christ, whose large rallies had surprised many, had fallen on hard times in France. Although the organization's work continued to expand in the United States and elsewhere in the world, the problems and scandal within the French organization darkened its reputation in France. It was not until the 1960's that Youth For Christ would again be active in France, but on a smaller scale and with a refurbished image.

The Youth For Christ movement was an inauspicious beginning for postwar American missionary work in France. The showy tactics so popular in Chicago grated upon French customs and sensitivity. The influx of American affluence cast the struggling French evangelicals in a poor light, or into the shadows. The French evangelicals felt that the Americans should have consulted them and cooperated with them. From the start, the French began to resent American missionary activity which they viewed as naive, insensitive, or even arrogant. The early contacts between the American missionaries and the French evangelicals were marked more by muted discord than by harmony. In subsequent years many of the misunderstandings and even differences would be reconciled, but some of the problems of the 1940's would linger into the 1970's.

From time to time other American evangelistic teams toured through France. The best-organized and most publicized were the Billy Graham campaigns of

1955 and 1963. Lesser known missions like the European Evangelistic Crusade, the Navigators, the Pocket Testament League, Operation Mobilization, and Youth With A Mission came and went. It was difficult to ascribe lasting results due to itinerant evangelism alone. Some of the groups employed little strategy other than "sowing the seed" of Christianity, hoping that somewhere, somehow it would grow.

The immediate postwar years saw several other American missions decide to send personnel to France. One of these missionaries arrived in France for the second time. The European Christian Mission, later called the Bible Christian Union was the only major American evangelical mission to have supported a missionary in France before the war. Harvey Phelps had worked in Paris shortly before the war and during the first year of the German occupation. Then he had fled to the unoccupied region of France and from there to the United States. During the war the European Christian Mission, through its periodical Europe's Millions, kept its constituency informed about plans to send missionaries to France as soon as conditions permitted. Phelps and his wife Della arrived in France in November 1946, having sailed across the Atlantic on the liner Ile de France, still equipped as a troop carrier. Disembarking in Cherbourg, Phelps boarded the crowded train for Paris, and then traveled south to Marseille where he attempted to pick up the threads of the evangelism effort he had been forced to abandon during the war.

The postwar work began with street meetings in the busy section of the city known as the Old Port. Preaching on the quai, Phelps was pleased by the number who would stop to listen. He noticed an interest in religious discussions which had not been apparent before, but which would diminish in the early 1950's.[33] In his reports to the office in America he described his daily work: "Many of those who attend the meetings are Italian, but they understand the French language. The women and children come from the poorest type of home, a fact to which their faded, worn clothing and their pale, pinched faces bear testimony."[34] Phelps organized the converts from these meetings into Bible Study groups which met in apartments, and within a year he had baptized twelve new converts. Then he decided to organize an evening Bible school. In America the Bible school movement had grown to become a vital aspect of evangelical

30

Christianity. Almost all large American cities, as well as many smaller ones, had at least one Bible institute. Phelps, like other evangelicals, was distressed by the small number of institutions in France at which men and women might receive evangelical instruction about the Scriptures. The little evening school which Phelps started met in a spare room in a home for working girls. Attendance approached twentyfive, and the European Christian Mission claimed its work in France reestablished.

Another American mission agency became involved in France soon after the war through unforeseen circumstances. Baptist Mid-Missions, an Ohio-based organization of fundamentalist and separatist persuasion, commissioned a large force of missionaries on several continents. At the end of the war the mission decided to send a few missionaries to recently liberated eastern Europe. Daniel Feryance, Arthur Sommerville, and Bernice Inman worked as missionaries in Czechoslovakia for less than a year when the communist seizure of power in 1948 forced them to leave. Hoping to continue their work with eastern Europeans, the missionaries traveled to Paris, where they bode their time by working with Slavic refuges. And they wondered what to do next. After assessing the religious climate of Paris, they decided that France needed missionaries as much as anywhere, and they opted to remain. Soon they were joined by three additional missionaries from the United States, and then all the Baptist Mid-Missions personnel in France moved to Bordeaux.

In their decision to choose Bordeaux as the site of their work, they were influenced by Jacques Blocher, the prominent French evangelical who was associated with the Paris Tabernacle Church and with the Nogent Bible Institute. He described Bordeaux as a "needy city" with almost no evangelical activity. He also realized that by encouraging the Americans to go to distant Bordeaux, he would force them to be independent, not relying upon him for aid. At that time the French evangelicals in Paris were not anxious to have another American mission establish itself in their city. The missionaries, finding the description of the religious situation in Bordeaux to be all too accurate, suffered from their inexperience and their isolation from the evangelical community of Paris.[35]

31

The Americans had little idea of how to proceed, and they made several blunders. Although the missionaries had not yet completed their language study, they attempted some tent evangelism, awkwardly using an interpreter. The results were negligible. Tent evangelism, born on the American frontier, was not attractive to Frenchmen who associated religion with cathedrals. Furthermore, the Americans chose sites for their tents which did not invite even the curious. The initial campaigns were held in tiny rural villages outside Bordeaux. The conservative villagers, fearful of what their nighbors might think, were reluctant to attend. Finally, under the cover of darkness, some elderly peasants snuck into the empty tent and stood in the shadows in the back. The failure of the tent campaign was followed by a similarly ill-conceived decision to open a mission hall in urban Bordeaux in early 1949. At first the missionaries did not realize that their building stood in the middle of the red light district, a neighborhood in which prospective church-goers were not likely to be found. The missionaries found it difficult to attract people to evangelical meetings in a former brothel. Furthermore, the missionaries all lived together, just as the Baptist Mid-Missions workers in Africa lived in a mission compound. Relying upon financial aid from the home office, the mission in Bordeaux purchased a hall, chairs, hymn books, etc. before there were any people to use them.[36] Concerned primarily with their evangelistic goals, the missionaries were not sensitive to French culture. Their work was based upon American money and the preconceptions of American fundamentalism. They were ill-advised in their attempt to transplant to Bordeaux missionary methods designed for Africa. Although some contacts had been made and some Bible studies begun, the enterprise was off to a weak start.

An early American missionary endeavor in postwar France whose impact was somewhat wider than the small number of its personnel might indicate was that of the Child Evangelism Fellowship, with its main offices in Grand Rapids, Michigan. In February 1949, the first Child Evangelism fellowship missionary arrived in France, and began to hold outdoor Bible classes for French youngsters. The mission's programs did not win quick acceptance. The basic concept of the evangelization of children met resistance in France, where infant baptism and first communion were usually thought to fulfill the church's role to children.

32

Another problem arose when some French Protestant churches proved reluctant to open their doors to children reached through street classes or clubs; the church Sunday School traditionally had been for the children of church members only. By 1975 Child Evangelism Fellowship in France had become a multinational organization with American presence continually diminished, and the salaries of the French assistants (meager as they were) exceeded that of the American directress. The program had grown to the point where it enrolled over 5,000 children in 176 groups throughout France.[37]

Most of the American missions in France became involved to some degree in the evangelism of children. Missionaries who felt uneasy in a new culture often found it more satisfying and less demanding to work with children rather than with adults. Some missionaries made it their central task. Most missionaries, however, viewed child evangelism not as an objective in itself, but as a means to reach the parents. Eventually most missions could point to adult converts who were initially contacted through their children. But by the 1970's a few missionaries questioned this approach. The attempt to persuade a little child to renounce the family religion (or the family's opposition to religion) could provoke great opposition. It made the missionaries appear to be intent on dissolving the French family unit. This impression, they concluded, rendered child evangelism an unproductive if not counter-productive activity.

The most significant accomplishment of the initial phase of postwar missionary work in France was the establishment of the European Bible Institute. The summer of 1948 found Robert Evans deeply troubled. Having worked with Youth For Christ in France for over a year, he was frustrated by the superficial impact of mass evangelism. Youth For Christ's demonstrated inability to retain converts, and its patently American flavor seemed to be increasingly limiting its effectiveness. Evans became convinced that a European country could be evangelized only by Europeans themselves, and that Americans could most effectively make their contribution by providing the evangelical instruction which was lacking in the French-speaking world. Evans and his wife, Jeanette, toured the American midwest for several months, attempting to raise money for a Bible school in Paris. In 1949 they decided to return to France and lay the ground work.

They arrived empty-handed. All their possessions were stolen from their Chevrolet station wagon as it was parked on a New York street the night before they embarked. Intending to start a school, they had no property, no teachers, and no students. The American couple moved into Paris discouraged but determined. Seeking out former Parisian acquaintances, Evans gathered a small group of young adults who were interested in serious and scholarly Bible study. For the remainder of 1949 the informal classes met in Evans' apartment. In 1950 he opened an evening school in university rooms in the Latin quarter. Meeting two nights a week, the school attracted students from a wide variety of backgrounds, including professional people as well as some from the working class. An international group representing almost a dozen nations, the student body increased from about twenty at the beginning of the year to over fifty by the end.[38] Evans did much of the instruction himself, although part-time help was donated by Daniel Feryance of Baptist Mid-Missions and several other newly-arrived Americans attached to other missions.

The school's financial position became increasingly insecure, and Evans was forced to seek new sources of support. Leaving his wife and young daughter in Paris, he returned to the United States where it took him over nine months of travel and speaking to raise the necessary funds. Although many individuals expressed a keen interest in the project, Evans was discouraged to find resistance from some prominent American evangelical leaders.[39] Some seemed more anxious to send missionaries to former enemies Germany and Japan than to their former French ally. Most American evangelicals felt that the French had lost their chance, or that France was too decadent ("Sodom on the Seine"), or that the French were distracted from Christianity by being always wearily bogged down in insolvable political problems.[40]

Even more discouraging was the opposition of French evangelical leaders. Although the evening school had been received politely by the French evangelical community, the plans for a full-time Bible institute were opposed vigorously. The French evangelicals worried about the new American competition with French institutions, and they resented the supposed affluence of the Americans. Part of the problem stemmed from the way in which the recent problems with Youth For Christ had tarnished the image of American missions. Some French critics assumed erroneously that there was a formal affiliation between Youth For Christ and the new Bible institute. The aggressive missionaries were not attuned to the concerns of the French evangelicals. It took at least five years for the American-run school even to begin to overcome French suspicion. Ultimately it was the graduates who began to dispel some of the doubts as the institute slowly won acceptance and was eventually recognized by the French evangelicals as an integral and valuable part of their community.

The success of the evening school encouraged Evans to seek additional full-time faculty as well as a building to house the institute. By the end of 1951 the mission completed arrangements to purchase an old building in suburban Chatou, about ten miles west of Paris, under the French name of the organization, the Ligue Biblique Francaise.[41] The building was large enough to meet the school's current needs, but it stood in disrepair. There was no electricity, heat had to be coaxed from an ancient furnace trying to burn coal dust, and the plumbing was limited to a single faucet in the kitchen. The floors and walls were covered with ink stains (the building formerly housed a Catholic elementary school) which the missionaries and students removed by scraping with pieces of broken glass. As funds and time became available, the rooms were restored one by one.[42]

By the end of 1951 the European Bible Institute had acquired not only a building, but also a tiny faculty. Irene Bonjour came from the staff of South Carolina's Columbia Bible College, and then she and the Evans were joined by Irishman Robert Munn and his wife. From its inception the European Bible Institute advertised itself as an international school. Its curriculum was bi-lingual, with courses offered in both French and English, a visionary step anticipating the growth of English as the lingua franca of the postwar world. Consequently, students from France were joined by those from all parts of the globe. The curriculum of the institute followed the pattern of three-year Bible schools in the United States, institutions which were designed to provide Biblical training for Christian workers and pastors who did not desire the academic preparation and rigor associated with theological seminaries.

The European Bible Institute officially inaugurated its Chatou building on January 15, 1952. Although the evening school continued to provide instruction for those students with daytime jobs, the main thrust of the school was its regular day curriculum in which nine students were enrolled for the first year. Seven were in the French section, and two were in the English section.

But the financial foundation of the institute continued to be unstable. The five missionaries agreed to donate half of their annual salaries to keep the school functioning for the first two years. However, that was not enough, and the school tottered on the brink of financial collapse. Heavily dependent upon the generosity of American evangelicals, the missionaries found it necessary for at least one of them to return annually to the United States in order to raise support for the school. The dependence of the school upon transfusions of American money tested and proved the faith of the American missionaries. But it also exacerbated the tensions between the American missionaries and the French evangelicals. The French assumed that the money came to the Americans more easily than it did, and they continued to feel that the new school was intended to compete with rather than complement their older and poorer institutions. Furthermore, the institute in Chatou, perhaps unavoidably, became a magnet for new American missionary personnel arriving in France. This gave rise to critical remarks about an "American missionary compound," and made it even more difficult for the Americans to win acceptance by the French.

However, the school doubled its enrollment in the second term, and within two years thirty students registered in the evening and day divisions.[43] Eventually the institute would outgrow its Chatou building and move to a former chateau in Lamorlaye, thirty miles north of Paris, near Chantilly. Refurbished by the missionaries themselves, the Lamorlaye campus of the European Bible Institute would be dedicated in October 1960, an event to be covered on French national television.[44] Buoyed by the success of the institute, and hopeful of an expanded future, Evans changed the name of his organization to the Greater Europe Mission in 1952.

The establishment of the European Bible Institute marked a significant milestone in the course of

American evangelical work in France. It signified a
definite sense of purpose and a settling-down which
came after the sometimes frantic and ill-conceived
evangelistic campaigns of the immediate postwar years.
The American missionaries plowed into France aggressively, and stepped on a few toes. The French evangelicals, in most cases impoverished in comparison
with the Americans, questioned the wisdom of American
spending policies. They resented American "surveys"
and publicity which tended to discount the existence
of any evangelical Christianity in France.[45] And
when the new American connection lured some young
French evangelicals to careers in America, church
leaders in France wondered if the American missionary
effort would result in a net loss for evangelicals in
France. Some lessons had been learned on both sides,
some had not. French society as a whole was unaware
of the small missionary presence.

CHAPTER II NOTES

[1]H. Godin, _La France: Pays de Mission_ (Paris: Ed. Abeille, 1943).

[2]Michael Novak, "Christianity: Renewed or Slowly Abandoned," in McLoughlin, p. 384.

[3]World Council of Churches, "Evangelism in France," Ecumenical Studies (Geneva: 1951) p. 1.

[4]_Ibid_.

[5]Kenneth Scott Latourette, _The Christian World Mission in Our Day_ (New York: Harper Brothers, 1954), p. 74; Marty, _Varieties of Unbelief_, p. 101; See also Dansette, II, 12, 15; David A. Shank, "Missionary Approach to a Dechristianized Society" _Mennonite Quarterly Review_, vol. XXXVIII, Jan. 1954, p. 40.

[6]World Council of Churches, p. 2.

[7]Jacques Ellul, _The New Demons_ (New York: Seabury Press, 1975), p. 24.

[8]_Ibid._, p. 25.

[9]E. E. Hayles, _The Catholic Church in the Modern World_ (Garden City, N.Y.: Hanover House, 1958), pp. 232-235; McManners, pp. 131, 171.

[10]International Congress on World Evangelism, France (_Status of Christianity Country Profile_). (Lausanne, 1974) p. 3.

[11]_Ibid._, p. 3; World Council of Churches, p. 2.

[12]World Council of Churches, p. 3; International Congress on World Evangelization (Lausanne 1974), p. 3. See also Godin, and Boulard, _op. cit._

[13]For corroborative comparison with Italy see Edward Banfield, _The Moral Basis of a Backward Society_ (Chicago: The University of Chicago Free Press, 1958), pp. 113, 130; Roger Hedlund, _The Protestant Movement in Italy_ (South Pasadena: William CArey Library, 1970), p. 32.

[14]International Congress on World Evangelization (Lausanne, 1974), p. 4.

[15]Ibid., p. 5.

[16]Coutrot & Dreyfus, p. 317; Robert, p. 4.

[17]Ibid., p. 113; Stuart Schram, Protestantism and Politics in France (Alencon: Corbiere and Jugian, 1954) p. 29; Dansette, II, p. 24.

[18]Lausanne Conference on World Evangelism, p. 6; Ronald Hoyle, "A Survey of Religion in Twentieth Century France," unpublished Master's thesis, Columbia Bible College, 1956), pp. 43-45.

[19]La Federation Protestante de France, La France Protestante (Valence: Imprimeries Réunies, 1956). See also 1967 edition.

[20]Reformed Evangelical News Exchange, vol. XVI, no. 11, Nov. 6, 1979, p. 1507; Dansette, II, pp. 24, 54, 262.

[21]Schram, op. cit.

[22]Martin, p. 123; Latourette, Christianity in a Revolutionary Age, vol. IV, pp. 378-379.

[23]Evans, Let Europe Hear, p. 153.

[24]Interview with Jacques Blocher, June 15, 1973.

[25]Stephan, p. 229.

[26]Saillens, p. 20; Stephan, p. 298.

[27]James Hefley, God Goes to High School (Waco, Texas: Word Books, 1970), p. 16.

[28]Hefley, p. 20.

[29]Hefley, p. 26.

[30]World Council of Churches, p. 17; Interview with Robert Evans, March 6, 1973.

[31]Interview with Rodney Johnston, director of Young Life in France, July 15, 1972.

[32]Hefley, p. 64.

[33]The previously cited World Council of Churches analysis of religion in postwar France agrees with the evangelical consensus that there seemed to be more interest in religion immediately after the war than in subsequent years. See also, C. Bishop, France Alive (New York: McMullen, 1947).

[34]Europe's Millions, November, 1947, p. 7; May 1948, p. 12, European Christian Mission, Brooklyn, N.Y.

[35]Interviews with Daniel Fereyance, June 12, 1973, and Bernice Inman, August 21, 1972.

[36]Interviews with Daniel Feryance, June 12, 1973, and Bernice Inman, August 21, 1972.

[37]France National Annual reports 1973-1974 and 1974-1975, Child Evangelism Fellowship.

[38]Robert Evans, Newsletter, June 1951, in files of Greater Europe Mission, Wheaton, Illinois.

[39]Letter from Noel Lyons, American director of European Bible Institute to the Board of Directors, September 6, 1950, Greater Europe Mission, Wheaton, Illinois.

[40]Evans, Let Europe Hear, p. 109.

[41]Letters from Noel Lyons to European Bible Institute Board, September 14, 1951 and September 26, 1951, Greater Europe Mission, Wheaton, Illinois.

[42]Robert Munn, "Profiles of Grace," unpublished manuscript on the history of the European Bible Institute, 1973, p. 2; R. Campbell, "Thirtieth Anniversary of EBI," European Reporter, GEM, March 1982, p. 6.

[43]Robert Munn, pp. 3, 4, 8.

[44]Reporter, GEM. April, 1960, p. 2; April 1961, pp. 8-11.

[45]John Young, "Survey of Evangelism in French-Speaking Europe," paper read to Foreign Workers Conference, September 1970, p. 6.

CHAPTER III

THE FIRST WAVE, 1950 - 1955

French society was troubled as it prepared to enter the 1950's. The promise and hope which accompanied the liberation from German oppression rapidly disintegrated into frustration and despair. The United States and Soviet Union, former allies during the Second World War, squared off as adversaries in the Cold War. European nations became political battlegrounds in a global clash of ideologies, and many Europeans feared that once again large armies would be locked in combat upon their still war-ravaged lands. In France political bitterness, economic malaise, and budding colonial conflict immobilized the government. The Fourth Republic was no improvement over the Third.

Rapidly approaching the brink of chaos, France avoided economic collapse and political paralysis only because of the massive aid sent from the United States under the Marshall Plan. However, although the French weathered the immediate crises of the late 1940's, the optimism and sustained economic growth which took root even in defeated Germany remained absent from France. Many French citizens felt excluded from the modest economic recovery, and large numbers of voters became disenchanted with the regime of squabbling politicians. Existentialism and philosophies of despair became entrenched in intellectual circles, and this contributed to a growing national climate of irresolution.

Official American concern about France manifested itself in the growing stream of technicans, advisors, businessmen, and military personnel which flowed into France to confront its political and economic problems. The American evangelical missionaries arriving at the same time were concerned solely with the religious condition of France. The French who came into contact with the missionaries were not quick to discern this important difference between the missionaries and the rest of the new American invasion, and tended to lump them all together.

Several distinguishing features marked American missionary work in France in the early and mid-1950's. Most important, the number of missionaries in France rose sharply. In 1950 the Missionary Research Library

in New York, then the leading authority on North
American Protestant missionary statistics, made a
survey of the distribution of missionaries throughout
the world. They reported none in France or anywhere
in Europe for that year. Obviously the figures
reached by the survey were incomplete. By 1958 a
similar study listed fifty-seven workers in France,
and there were at least sixty who went unreported.
The most rapid increase came between 1952 and 1956
when missionary candidates finished their post-war
education, and then sailed for France. It was almost
impossible to derive the exact number of missionaries
in France, or anywhere else, at a particular time.
Two issues clouded the statistics: furloughs and
wives. Each year some of the missionaries reported
assigned to France were actually on furlough in
America for varying lengths of time. The problem
concerning wives stemmed from their uncertain place in
a missionary census. Although a few mission agencies
did not count missionary wives when numbering their
personnel, most did include married women even if
their duties were confined to homemaking. Many of
these American women in foreign lands found all their
time consumed by caring for the home and children.
Others, however, also assumed tasks more directly
related to the mission's religious activity. Missionary rosters did not distinguish function. At any
rate, the majority of the officially counted American
missionary force in France was female, because most
missionaries were couples, most missions counted
wives, and among the single missionaries, women far
outnumbered the men.

Second, the Americans had not yet successfully
convinced the French evangelicals that missionary work
in France was necessary, although some progress on
this was being made. Economics caused problems. The
French evangelicals contended that the amount of money
used to support one American could support two or even
three French evangelical workers, and the French were
convinced that they would be far more successful in
evangelizing their own countrymen than would foreigners.[1] It was even more difficult for the missionaries to justify their work to the average Frenchman,
especially in these early years when many missionaries
referred to themselves as such, rather than using the
term "pastor" as became their practice later. To most
modern Frenchmen the term "missionary" conjured up
images of colonialism, tropical countries, and exotic

foreign peoples. They saw no place for a missionary in France.

Third, there was little or no coordination between these American evangelical missions who were setting up operations in France. Even though the missionaries from different organizations held the same faith, sought the same goals, and worked in the same area, each group termed its work a "pioneer ministry", and usually chose to remain uninvolved with other missions. The concept of a pioneer ministry, transplanted to France from the American West and from mission fields in Africa or Asia, did little to help bridge the gap between the French evangelicals and the newly arrived Americans. American missions were slow to realize that France was a different sort of mission field. Some mission executives even contemplated merely patterning their personnel distribution in France according to a plan devised for missions in China. As late as the mid-1970's several American missions continued to refer to their work in France as pioneer work, a testimony to the persistent tendency of the American missionaries to disregard the ancient Christian heritage of France.[2]

Fourth, the missionaries gradually withdrew from Paris proper as their main field of activity, and took up residence in the suburbs or elsewhere in France. Economics, especially the cost of rent, may have been a factor here (certainly it would make work within the center of Paris almost prohibitively expensive by the 1960's) but the very size of the capital city prompted the missionaries to live elsewhere. Some said that Paris seemed almost too large and too intimidating to handle. However, the areas to which they moved, especially the suburbs in the departments of Seine-et-Marne and Seine-et-Oise, had been pegged as resistant to religion as early as the eighteenth century.[3]

Fifth, throughout the 1950's the evangelical community in the United States slowly became more completely informed about the religious climate of France as articles on the subject appeared in widely read evangelical periodicals.[4] Consequently the decision to send missionaries to France raised fewer eyebrows in American evangelical circles.

Sixth, arriving in France with unbridled optimism, the Americans very quickly became discouraged. The methods and gimmicks which had proved to be successful evangelistic aids in the United States usually failed in France. Convinced at first that the job of evangelizing France could be completely accomplished in a decade, the success-oriented Americans were forced to come to terms with under-achievement. Jacques Blocher, a French evangelical to whom Americans occasionally turned for assistance, had recounted the story of one optimistic American who came to him just before initiating a summer campaign of tent evangelism. The missionary wanted to know what he should do with all of the converts at the end of the summer. Blocher advised him to wait and see. In October the missionary wrote that there had been only one convert. Blocher replied that it usually took time for Americans to understand the religious situation in France.[5] Discouraged by their slow progress in French culture, the American missionaries generally concluded that the work and time necessary to produce one convert in France would yield ten or even twenty in the United States.

Finally, the American evangelical missionaries slowly became an informal but definite group. Shortly after his arrival in Paris, Robert Evans had started an English-speaking evangelical fellowship which was attended by other missionaries, as well as by American military, diplomatic, and business personnel in Paris. This was augmented by the establishment in 1953 of a regular Sunday worship service which he continued for several years at the Salle Pleyel in downtown Paris. More important in terms of establishing a sense of group solidarity, the American missionaries (along with a few British) convened their first annual Foreign Workers Conference at the European Bible Institute in Chatou in September 1952. These early group activities coalesced more or less haphazardly and spontaneously. Having no official sponsor, the first conference was organized through the combined efforts of the missions working in France. It became an annual event, scheduling speakers and panel discussions concerning the problems of missionary work in France. The change from year to year in the content of the papers delivered at the conference demonstrated the increasing cultural sophistication of the missionaries. At first the missionaries gave most of their attention to the technical aspects of their evangelistic methods: how to conduct a tent campaign, how to hang gospel bill posters, how to distribute literature, etc. Then, in the late 1950's the focus shifted to broad discussions of general evangelistic strategies, with missionary spokesmen from different missions presenting their views. By the late 1960's the focus settled upon the adaptation of the missionary and his message to French culture, with papers being read and discussions being chaired by French social scientists and pastors.[6] Another way in which the annual Foreign Workers Conference contributed to a sense of community among the missionaries in France was through the compilation of a directory of the Anglo-Saxon missionaries in French-speaking Europe. However, the invertebrate and dispersed nature of the missionary community meant there were several ommissions in each edition.

The degree to which the American missionaries in France had (or should) become a distinct group provoked sharp opinions. Some American and French evangelicals contended that the conference served only to underscore the foreign nature of the missionary activity in France, raising even higher the cultural barrier between the missionaries and the French. A few opponents even asserted that the conference offered the missionaries a convenient occasion to criticize the French. Others maintained that the meeting provided a needed opportunity for consultation about missionary methods in France, and that the successive meetings indicated progressive cultural awareness on the part of the missionaries.

In the early 1950's the European Bible Institute remained the primary example of American missionary work in France. Its enrollment growing slowly but steadily, with additional America personnel joining the faculty, the institute became a focal point and a source of aid for the other missionaries who had begun to arrive in France. The school became more widely known, both in France and in the United States. Founder Robert Evans' friend Billy Graham was beginning to become a national figure in America. Graham invited Evans to address a large campaign crowd in Houston, and continued to give his support to the school. Of greater importance, relations seemed to have improved slightly with French and other European evangelical leaders.[7]

While the European Bible Institute was still the only site of the Greater Europe Mission's work, the basic educational ministry branched out to include radio broadcasting and gospel billposting. David Barnes, who had come to France with the Evangelical

Alliance Mission (TEAM), supervised the radio work which began in a studio constructed in the former wine cellar of the institute. However, the impact of evangelical radio programs in France was limited severely because commercial stations usually aired the programs only between midnight and six in the morning.[8]

The gospel billposting project struggled with a similarly narrow impact. The gospel posters displayed a Bible verse and a brief message, and offered a New Testament to anyone who wrote for one. By the 1960's the mission printed and posted over 20,000 posters annually. Some of these remained in place for as long as one year, while others were torn down or papered over within several hours.[9]

Evaluation of a project of this sort proved difficult, although from time to time the missionaries at the Bible Institute received letters from Frenchmen who had made a Christian commitment because of the message of a poster. One such man subsequently attended the institute. The project was not without problems, and one early incident illustrated the difficulties which missionaries encountered within secularized French culture. A missionary went to a printer's shop and placed an order for posters with a quotation from the New Testament: "The wages of sin is death." (Romans 6:23). The printer insisted that the word for sin -- péché -- did not exist. An argument ensued, although the missionary left the shop thinking that he had convinced the printer. Later he returned to find thousands of posters with the inscription: "The wages of fishing -- pêche -- is death." The importance the missionaries ascribed to billposting was highest in the early years, perhaps because in those years the billposting project was one of the few activities in which they could busy themselves.

The urge to establish institutes captured the minds of some missionaries from Baptist Mid-Missions. After having organized a small church group in Bordeaux, the missionaries decided to open a Bible school. The Baptist Mid-Missions attempt in Bordeaux did not achieve even the modest success of the European Bible Institute in Chatou. The Bordeaux Bible School, in operation by 1954, never had many students (sometimes two or three, never more than six), but was costly because it tied up the time of five missionaries and necessitated expenditures for the school

46

building. The school's inability to achieve success became a source of contention within the mission, and the Baptist Mid-Missions work in France was plagued by dissension and loss of personnel. Eventually the moribund school was phased out in 1961.

The decision to start a Bible school would be repeated by mission after mission during the next twenty years of American missionary work in France. The multiplication of these tiny Bible schools reflected the desire of each mission agency to promote and protect zealously its particular theological emphasis. However, the very small pool of potential students for the schools placed them in competition with each other, dooming some to rapid extinction and the others to a dwarfed existance. It all served to underscore the sectarian and even factious nature of the American missionary effort in France.

The early 1950's saw not only the continuation of the missionary work begun in the 1940's, but also the initial decisions of other American mission agencies to send personnel to France. Some worldwide missions added France to an already extensive list of mission fields. Other mission societies directed their effort solely to Europe, or even to France alone. Some were large interdenominational missions dealing in millions of dollars and thousands of missionaries around the globe. A few were very small, run by parttime volunteer administrators with an office amounting to little more than a file cabinet in a midwestern apartment.

The Navigators, a service mission which provided aid to evangelical churches in several countries in the form of Bible memory work, teaching materials, and evangelism, sent George Clark and David Roher to France. At first, neither had much of a plan, but eventually Clark was able to build up an extensive network of relationships within the evangelical community in France. Marrying a French woman, and becoming well assimilated into French society, Clark would in 1962 become the head of the French office of the Billy Graham Evangelistic Association, and become one of the most widely-known evangelicals in France.

Another mission whose stated aims were evangelism and service to French churches was the European Evangelistic Crusade, a strongly fundamentalist movement founded by a Scotsman, James Stewart.[10] Propelled

47

largely by the forceful pesonalities of its founder and his brother Douglas, the European Evangelistic Crusade very quickly became one of the largest missions in Europe. Although missionaries from this organization moved into France in 1950, the French effort was never as large as those in Eastern Europe, Germany, Italy and the Netherlands. In the early 1950's the somewhat haphazard work of the European Evangelistic Crusade in France included holding evangelistic meetings for children, distribution of CARE packages, and efforts in tent evangelism.[11]

A more definite missionary program occupied the American Mennonites. The Mennonite Central Committee, a relief agency composed of representatives from different Mennonite churches, had become involved in several reconstruction programs in postwar France. This mission traditionally focused on social and physical rehabilitation, not evangelism. The Mennonites supervised food distribution projects, and they provided substantial aid to French Mennonites in the rebuilding of war-damaged churches and homes. Less than six months after VE Day, fourteen American Mennonites labored in relief projects in France.[12] In the difficult year of 1947, when harsh living conditions nearly crippled Europe, the Mennonites distributed twenty-one tons of food and clothing to needy French citizens.[13] By 1950 the Mennonite Central Committee work in France was limited almost entirely to the operation of two children's homes at Nancy and Weiler in eastern France. Then the Nancy home was transferred to Valdoie, a property near Belfort which was purchased jointly by the French Mennonites and the Mennonite Central Committee. Control of both homes shifted gradually to the French Mennonites.[14] As the Mennonite Central Committee phased out its postwar relief programs, a new mission work was planned by another Mennonite agency, the Mennonite Board of Missions and Charities, located in Elkhart, Indiana. They aimed to strengthen the French Mennonites who were organized in a score of congregations in eastern France and in Paris. Although the mission also had aims for general evangelism, their decision to establish a close partnership with extant French churches of their own creed would distinguish Mennonite missions from those of the other evangelicals. It was a wise decision. By assuming a fraternal position beside the French Mennonites, the Americans avoided many of the problems of cultural conflict which plagued the relations between most

American mission agencies and the French evangelicals. The Mennonite missionary effort remained small, but would develop successfully. It was low key, but in tune with its French colleagues.

Alerted to the religious needs of France (and those of the French Mennonites in particular) while doing relief work in Belgium, Orley Swartzentruber and his wife moved to Paris on the last day of 1953. Swartzentruber had grown up in Argentina, the son of Mennonite missionaries to that country. Taking up residence in the southern suburbs, Swartzentruber began to seek out the few Mennonites living in the Paris region. Before long he gathered a small group of ten or fifteen which met regularly for Bible study. As the group grew it became more difficult to find places to meet. For while in 1955 Swartzentruber resorted to holding the weekly service in a rented bus. The next year the group formally constituted itself as a church, though with only three members; they and about thirty who regularly attended collected funds to erect a tiny prefabricated meeting hall on land which the mission had purchased in the community of Butte Rouge.[15] However, Swartzentruber became discouraged by the group's small size and its inability to attract men. This was not unusual. Evangelical groups seemed to meet the religious interest and social needs of women more readily than those of men. Women signficantly outnumbered men in missionary groups and churches, and the lack of male leadership kept many groups small. The situation became a vicious circle, for as more women joined the groups, it seemed increasingly less likely that men would join. The American missionaries were committed to the principal of male church leadership by custom and doctrine. They carved out only small public roles for female missionaries and parishioners alike.

As other American evangelical mission boards began to turn their attention toward France in the early 1950's, the number of missonaries working there grew, a couple at a time. In November 1951 Frederick Fogle and his wife arrived in Paris to begin language studies. They were the first missionaries to France sent by the Foreign Missionary Society of the National Fellowship of Brethren Churches. This evangelical denomination, commonly known as the Grace Brethren, found most of its adherents in the American midwest where it operated a college and seminary at Winona Lake, Indiana. The mission had been encouraged to send personnel to France by missionaries bound for Africa who were studying in Paris. They came to the conclusion shared by others that France deserved as much missionary attention as did her colonies. In Janaury 1953 Fogle moved to Lyon where he began the task of gathering together a group of evangelicals. Plodding through the streets, knocking on doors, he very slowly made contact with a number of interested people through tract distribution, door-to-door visitation, children's classes, and adult home Bible study. Subsequently he established a preaching center in downtown Lyon, and made plans to organize the people into church later in the decade.[16]

The Plymouth Brethren expanded their small and unobtrusive mission work in France as local assemblies in America undertook the support of workers in suburban Paris and Vichy.[17] An organization in New York, Christian Missions in Many Lands, handled legal affairs and transferral of funds, but Plymouth Brethren missionaries were largely independent, responsible only to the North American assembly which had underwritten their support. Unlike most missions, the Plymouth Brethren made no rigid distinction between American missionaries and French Brethren. Funds raised in the United States were sent to French pastors as well as to American missionaries.[18] The couple in Vichy were an example of the mixed nationalities of the Brethren mission. Trifon and Priscilla Kalioudjoglou were both born in France, although Priscilla was raised in the United States. Her support came from a Brethren assembly in Chicago, while his came from groups in Lyon and in Vichy.[19]

Another small missionary venture which started in the early 1950's was that of the Slavic Gospel Association, a mission whose goal was to carry evangelical Christianity to Eastern Europe, especially the Soviet Union. The work in France assumed two forms: (1) work among Slavic refugees, and (2) the construction of a supply center from which forays were made into the eastern bloc countries. This group's missionary in France, William Kapitaniuk, assumed responsibility for a Polish church in the northern French industrial town of Billy Montigny where the mission set up its base of operations.

The most significant missionary arrival in France in the early 1950's was Arthur P. Johnston, the first worker to be sent to France by the Evangelical

Alliance Mission, more commonly known as TEAM. The first large interdenominational American mission to enter France, TEAM was recognized as an important force in the worldwide evangelical missionary movement. Founded in 1890 by Frederick Fransen as the Scandanavian Alliance Mission of North America, this organization had quickly developed a global commitment with deep involvement in China. Although the communist victory in China rendered missionary work there impossible, TEAM expanded its work to other Asian states and to Africa. By 1975 TEAM, with an annual income of six million dollars, would sponsor over 1,000 missionaries in twenty-two nations. Its international ministry would include churches, Sunday schools, radio stations, hospitals, secondary schools, colleges, theological seminaries, and publishing houses.[20] TEAM's interest in France began with a visit to Paris in 1950 by General Director David H. Johnson. After reading Johnson's report -- "A person born in France has less opportunity to hear the Gospel and be saved than one born in the heart of Africa" -- the mission decided to send missionaries to Europe.[21]

When Arthur Johnston and his wife Muriel arrived in Paris on January 26, 1952, they had little idea where to start. After completing his M.A. at Wheaton College in 1951, the tall, athletic, blond Minnesotan had originally planned a missionary career in Tibet. His interest has been diverted to France only six months before his arrival in Europe. Moving into an apartment in Paris' fifth arrondissement, Johnston enrolled in language study at the Alliance Francaise, and decided to organize a youth ministry. His brother Rodney joined him the next year, and the two men attempted to apply the methods of a Texas-bred movement known as Young Life. This organization, avoiding the image of the institutional church and speaking the youth idiom, had been successful in the United States by contacting young peole on athletic fields and in other youth haunts. Johnston's first contacts in France were with American teenagers in Paris with whom they played football and baseball in the Bois de Boulogne. The American teenagers brought their French friends to see the novel spectacle, and soon the Johnston brothers attempted to form a French Young Life club to complement the American Young Life club which they had already founded through contacts made at the American church in Paris.[22] But the Texas method did not transfer readily to France. French youth did not have the sports programs of American high schools nor did they tend to congregate outside the lycée after school. Again, the Americans found themselves separated from the French by cultural as well as theological differences. But by adapting their approach, and by doggedly pursuing relationships with French and American youth, the Johnston brothers eventually founded a French Young Life club in the fashionable sixteenth arrondissement of Paris by October 1953, with an average Saturday night attendance of thirty-five.[23]

In the meantime the work of TEAM in France began to expand, as much in contact with other Americans as with the French. Arthur Johnston accepted an invitation from Robert Evans to teach at the newly founded European Bible Institute, and additional missionaries began to arrive. David Barnes, who arrived with his wife in July 1952, had been a French instructor at the fundamentalist Bob Jones University in South Carolina, and therefore felt he could plunge into missionary work (an evangelistic tent campaign in St. Germain) without preliminary language study. Results were meager. Later in 1953 he worked with scant success as an itinerant evangelist in Bordeaux and Lyon. Barnes also was invited to teach at the European Bible Institute, and ultimately was asked to become its director when Evans resigned.[24] However, the invitation for Barnes to leave TEAM and join the Greater Europe Mission was proffered improperly, and the two American missions which later would become the largest in France got off together on the wrong foot.

By 1955 the work of TEAM in France was divided into two main parts, with a third aspect just beginning. The new work was thrust upon the missionaries in France when two TEAM missionaries in Spain, John and Betty Aerni, were expelled from that country. Determined to continue working with Spaniards, the Aernis settled in the southern city of Béziers where they planned to contact the sizable Spanish community.[26] This project, just under way in the mid-1950's, would limp along, the perennial weak sister of the TEAM mission to France.

The TEAM missionaries directed much of their energy toward the establishment of an evangelical group in the Paris suburb of Vitry-sur-Seine. The reason for the selection of this grimy industrial town was simply that it was there that the missionaries found housing. In this early era of mission work in France, missions fell into the practice of having their area of concentration decided for them by the availability of housing; the era of more thoughtful strategy still lay in the future. With the arrival of John and Ethel Jesberg in August 1953, there were four TEAM couples in France. Except for Arthur and Muriel Johnston, they all lived on the same street in Vitry. This did little to aid their assimilation into French society. Attempting to interest their neighbors in Christianity, they were politely received but often firmly rebuffed. Distribution of literature yielded little. Normally there was only one response per thousand leaflets.[27] Although few Frenchmen expressed open hostility, the missionaries became dis-couraged by the pervasive indifference to religion. But there was some progress. The first convert was a plumber who came to fix a leak in Arthur Johnston's home. A cleaning girl also professed to having become a believer, and subsequently a regular Bible study began in the missionary's apartment. But many who expressed interest, or even conversion, later dropped out. Inroads into French society came slowly. The missionaries had originally been regarded with suspi-cion in the heavily communist neighborhood, but slowly their status in the community changed from that of "the Americans" to that of "the American pastors." But the pastors in Vitry had no parish.[28]

The other part of the TEAM effort and still the primary focus in 1955, was the youth work, or Young Life club. The missionaries concentrated upon teen-agers because young people demonstrated an interest which was absent in adults. Also, the Americans' grasp of the French language was still inadquate, and the teenagers were more tolerant of (or intrigued by) their accents.[29] Plagued with continuing prob-lems, such as the difficulty in retaining a hall for regular meetings, the Johnston brothers were alter-nately encouraged and discouraged. A period of dwin-dling attendance would be followed by a dozen "professions of faith in Christ," and then another slump. Attempting to consolidate the young people into the church group, Arthur Johnston initiated a Sunday worship service for them in the Quaker Hall on Avenue Mozart. The first Young Life Summer Camp (Rodney Johnston and four boys in a station wagon) met in 1955. The Johnston brothers indulged in what proved to be unwarranted optimism. "It may be," one wrote, "that these fellow will be . . . the future leaders of the work in France.[30]

There remained, however, nagging doubts about the youth work. The group of about thirty-five needed ceaseless attention, and the missionaries realized that it was made up of teens who would very soon out-grow the Young Life club. After three years in France TEAM missionaries could point to some success (sixty professed conversions by 1954) but not nearly as much as they had anticipated. The initial expectation of enthusiastic response to evangelism had evaporated. TEAM began to be concerned about the image it was pro-jecting in France. Should the methods be changed? Should an official headquarters be established?[31] TEAM began to settle in for the long haul, but without knowing just how it was to be accomplished.

From the beginning, keeping in touch with the people at home was an important part of missionary work in France. When American missionaries went to France, even if for a lifetime of service, they did not cut themselves off from their homeland. Instead, each missionary maintained a multifaceted relationship with America which in many ways governed his or her work in France, and greatly influenced missionary participation in French society. Many times mission policies and practices reflected, not the situation in France, but the dictates of the home office, the sentiment in churches back home, the demand for missionary literature, and the furlough schedule.

The furlough was the most important aspect of the American connection. Each missionary returned regu-larly to the United States for periods ranging from three months to over one year. The furlough served several purposes. Most important was the strengthen-ing of the relationship between the missionaries and the Americans who provided their financial support. Churches and individual supporters tended to lose interest without personal contact with the missionary from time to time. Second, the missionaries desired to maintain the bonds with their own culture and its evangelical community, particularly for the sake of their children. Finally, furlough provided a chance for some to continue academic study.

54

Traditionally, American missionaries had served a four or five year term, followed by a one year furlough. This was the schedule most American missionaries in France followed in the postwar years, but toward the end of the 1960's some missions changed to a schedule of three month summer furloughs every two or three years. There were three reasons for this. First, it was made feasible by air transporation; the old schedules dated from the days when most missionaries had to make long sea voyages to Asia or Africa. Second, it did not interrupt the education of their children. Third, the inflationary spiral made it necessary to extend continually the base of financial support, even though summer was not the best time to find packed churches to hear a pitch.

For most missionaries furlough was a time for living out of a suitcase, driving from one speaking engagement to another, renewing the relationships with their constituents. Only a few drew their support from churches and individuals clustered in one area, so most missionaries found it necessary to travel to every region of the United States. Several times a week (sometimes several times a day) the missionaries stopped to speak at church services, women's luncheons, youth meetings, and especially missionary conferences. The usual format included a slide show, a report on the accomplishments of the previous term, and a plea to support the missionary effort. Enduring the ordeal of incessant travel, the missionary on furlough was nagged by the need to attain a specified amount of pledged support before returning to France. Since appeals for funds were normally indirect, the missionaries did not know for some time after a speaking engagement how much, if at all, those in attendance had been moved to give. Sometimes they were forced to delay their departure for France for weeks or months until the minimum support figures had been pledged. Although furlough was intended primarily as a time of financial, spiritual, and physical renewal, many missionaries participated as actively in evangelism as they had done in France. One indefatigable preacher held evangelistic meetings all but six days of his furlough, and claimed over one thousand "decisions for Christ."[32]

Furloughed missionaries from France faced problems unlike those of missionaries from more traditional fields in Africa and Asia. In spite of the growth of the missionary presence in France throughout the postwar years, it remained difficult to persuade American Christians that there was a great need for missionaries in European nations. Furthermore, missions in France did not grip the imagination like those from more distant cultures. The missionary conference slide show of concrete high-rise apartments in Sarcelles, long loaves of French bread, and tract distribution under the Eiffel tower seemed tame when the next speaker from New Guinea filled the screen with poisonous snakes, the head-hunter-turned-deacon, and mass baptism by a jungle stream. Interest and support went to the most exotic.[33] Some American evangelicals continued to display a special reluctance toward providing France with missionary aid. They held the opinion (not too clearly reasoned) that the French were too decadent, too sinful to deserve missionary help. On the other hand, a few missionaries affirmed that being a missionary to France actually placed them in a better position. When the novelty and curiosity factor of a missionary to France outweighed the lack of exciting pictures, the missionaries found that the usually surprised American listeners responded generously.[34]

The most important feature of the furlough was its impact upon the work of France. Although the missionaries were convinced that the work in France could be sustained only by the financial and emotional support gathered at home, the furlough system produced negative results in France. Returning to France often led to an emotional crisis of depression and soul-searching. After having been received warmly during their months within the evangelical community of America, the missionaries recoiled from the slow pace and chilling frustrations of the work in France. A more harmful effect of the furlough was the tendency of the work in France, so painstakingly built up over four or five years, to weaken or even collapse during the missionary's absence. Sometimes a project was formally discontinued when the missionary returned to the United States on furlough. At best, the missionaries covered furlough absences by shuffling personnel in France, causing transition problems, and doing little to convey the impression that their work was strongly based and permanent.

Since the financial connection between the missionary in France and his homeland assumed a priority role during furlough, a brief discussion of missionary finance is in order, although limited by a lack of reliable information. Most mission agencies with personnel in France termed themselves "faith missions." By this they intended to convey their conviction that faith in God would bring them the necessary funds, and therefore they sought no denominational affiliation for the purpose of guaranteeing support. Instead, they expected faithful believers in evangelical churches to give money to support the missonaries. This provided an opportunity for personal contact between the missionaries and their supporters, but it also placed the missionaries in the awkward position where they were accountable to supporting churches and individuals, as well as to their mission board.

Some missonaries received support from as many as sixty or seventy sources, whereas others, especially the Plymouth Brethren missionaries, looked to one church in the United States or Canada for their entire support. Of those who relied upon more numerous sources, a few depended primarily on a large number of individual donors, but most missionaries received over eighty percent of their support from churches. Some enrolled one or two large churches, while others accumulated smaller amounts from fifteen or twenty churches. Like the missionaries themselves, most of their financial support came from the midwest and middle Atlantic states.

Mission boards differed in the amount of support they required. Typical support figures including round-trip transportation, for instance, in the late 1960's amounted to $3,00 per year for a single missionary, and over $12,000 for a family of four or five; by the 1970's the devaluation of the dollar and the inflationary pressure in the French economy pushed the figures to nearly $5,000 and $20,000 respectively. Many missionary families were large (several included more than six children) and this required them to raise a considerable sum to insure even a modest standard of living. Some mission boards required more than others for insurance and retirement. In most cases a small percentage of each missionary's fund went to support the home office.

Missions also differed in their soliciting methods. Some issued frequent and detailed appeals for funds, especially when a specific project such as the construction of a church building necessitated a large expenditure. Other missions felt that a general statement of its aims in France would motivate people

to give. Still others, especially the Brethren, saw
no appeals for funds in the New Testament, and accordingly would not make their financial needs known,
trusting that God would prompt donors to give the
needed money for the missionaries and for special projects.[35] Sometimes Brethren missionaries found
employment in France. Or, to put it another way,
sometimes Brethren assemblies in the United States
offered financial support for the Christian work of
someone who already held employment in France.

When missionaries first went to France in the
late 1940's and early 1950's the amount of their
yearly support, although meager by American standards
(about $3,000 per couple) enabled them to live at the
level of the middle class in France, or even the upper
class, especially if they owned an automobile and the
usual household appliances which were common in America but rare in France. This is what led many French
evangelicals to say that the money used to support one
American missionary family could be better used in the
support of two or three full-time French Christain
workers. As the postwar economic recovery in France
gained momentum, French prices rose so sharply that by
the mid-1960's France became one of the most expensive
mission fields in the world.[36] Although the missionaries raised steadily the level of basic support,
the French standard of living rose so sharply that the
American missionaries felt they lived on the level of
the lower middle class or even the lower class.

The financial investment in the American evangelical missionary venture in France reflected the steady
rise in both the number of missionaries and the cost
of living. Uneven mission accounting practices make
it impossible to obtain figures indicating the total
investment, although partial figures may be helpful.
In 1953 the Chicago office of TEAM remitted to France
$14,218 originally contributed by the individual and
church supporters of each missionary. This figure
increased to $21,352 in 1958, $32,033 in 1963, $58,256
in 1968 and $202,803 in 1975. These figures do not
include money raised for housing and property
purchase, which could add over $40,000 to some
years.[37] Between 1960 and 1970 TEAM spent nearly
$1,000,000 in France.[38] Other missions showed
similar increases. For instance, the receipts from
the United States for the operating budget of the
Greater Europe Mission rose from $8,000 in 1953 to
$141,833 in 1970.[39] One mission leader estimated

that by the mid-1960's American missions had spent more than $3,000,000 in France.[40] The next decade swelled that figure by as much as another million.

Another important link in the chain connecting the missionary in France with his homeland was publication. This was an old tradition. Missionary literature played a role in shaping American culture. In an earlier period of American history, before international tourism and television became commonplace, the reports sent home by missionaries painted much of the picture Americans saw of foreign lands.[41]

The main goal of missionary publications was to convince the American evangelical community of the need for more extensive mission work in France. Since many American evangelical Christians remained lukewarm or even negative about France as a mission field, the consistent message of the public information concerned the lack of Christianity in France. There was little attempt to deal with the compelling larger issues of secularization, de-Christianization, and re-Christianization. Instead, for instance, published articles stressed the need to save French souls from the dangers presented by Communism ("The Rising Red Tide"), Roman Catholicism ("Local Priest Forbade Attendance at Missionary Children's Meeting"), alcoholism ("France: The Wettest Country in the World"), and sorcery ("Hundreds of Sorcerers in Normandy").[42] Articles frequently cited the appraisals of African pastors who said that France was more pagan than her former colonies.

In addition to providing general opinions about the religious needs of France, the missionary publicity focused upon two tangible objectives. First, the material shared with the supporters of missionary work was designed to elicit specific support in prayer and financial contribution. Second, the missionaries intended their publicity to interest new missionary candidates.[43] Three principal publication vehicles carried information about missionary work in France: periodic newsletters sent by individual missionaries, articles appearing in mission or denominational magazines, and a few books.

The newsletters, or "prayer letters" as they were usually called, supplied the most information and provided the most frequent source of contact. The letters were sent from four to six times a year. The

59

number of names on a missionary's mailing list varied
from twenty-five to nearly three thousand, with four
or five hundred being the average figure. A number of
these letters circulated within large churches so the
size of the constituency was often much larger than
the number on the mailing list. There was
considerable variety in the quality and quantity of
news presented. At the bottom of the scale were those
letters written in the babytalk genre. Each mission
seemed to have at least one missionary couple who
specialized in this strange form of communication.
Written as though by the youngest member of a
missionary family, these letters prattled on about the
activities of Poppa, Momma, and Big Brother and
Sister. Often this method was used when there was
nothing of substance to report.

The most common form of newsletter contained
reports of missionary accomplishment and requests for
prayer for certain projects and people, as seen in the
following excerpts.

> Jeanot's mother, a widow from Orly, prayed for
> his salvation every Wednesday in our prayer
> meeting. What a thrill to see this twenty-two
> year old dental technician come out boldly for
> Christ in the camp.[44]

*　　　　*　　　　*

> I was not sure where Elizabeth (age 18) stood.
> For a while she regularly attended our meet-
> ings until her parents hindered her from con-
> tinuing. Her conduct at the camp revealed a
> transformed life as she mixed with the others.
> Around the campfire she firmly confessed
> receiving Christ during the invitation given
> at one of our Orly meetings two years ago.
> Her brother Eric and I prayed for her many
> times.

*　　　　*　　　　*

> Yesterday, Jacques, 24, brought Fernand, 24,
> to the house. They spoke in glowing terms of
> what the camp meant to them. Jacques was saved
> several months ago, but Fernand revealed that
> just the night before he had asked Christ to be
> Saviour and Lord.[45]

*　　　　*　　　　*

60

Prayer was asked for a farmer and his wife. I
offered them a Gospel calendar with a daily
reading and they have found it a real source
of blessing. There is an obvious change in
his life. Pray for them. Another musician,
the saxaphonist at the Conservatory of Music,
has become very proud and self-sufficient.
But God may easily break this down one day and
he may once again listen to the claims of
Christ.[46]

A few were reluctant to mention their French contacts
by name:

Madame T. is more attracted to the Cathlic
church and hesitates to come with her husband,
but I feel that God is gently wooing her to
Himself. May she soon find true joy and salvation. Since last October a new lady, Madame
P., and her fifteen year old son have been
coming to meetings quite regularly.[48]

The anonymity of persons mentioned in the newsletter,
aside from being a gesture of polite discretion, was
due to an excessive fear expressed by some missionaries that newsletters would be read by American Catholic officials who would then send the names of people
mentioned to the local French priest, who might try to
forbid them to attend Protestant meetings.[48]

A few missionaries supplemented progress reports
of French Christians and potential converts with
informative essays about missionary work in France.
These correspondents routinely included comments upon
historical and contemporary influences which shaped
the French mind, including the philosophy of Teilhard
de Chardin, the Napoleonic legacy, and the French
school system.

Although newsletters were the richest and most
personal source of public information about the
missionary work in France, they probably were not the
most widely read form of publicity. Articles printed
in the magazines published by individual mission
boards reached a wider audience. Some of these journals maintained a circulation of over 40,000. The
initial aim of these articles was to impress upon the
readers the great need for missionary work in France.
Although immediately after the war a few articles
dealt with the material and political needs of the

61

French, the main concern was religious.[49] In fact, sometimes the two were set in contrast, as in a 1951 article in the Grace Brethren Herald: "Recently the plans of our government have been to send at least six billion dollars to Europe to save it from Communism. How much will the Brethren Church send to save it from Hell? Communism is bad enough, but an eternity in Hell is much worse."[50]

The extent of de-Christianization was underscored by citing the opinions of French church authorities and secular scholars. The opinion of D. W. Brogan that "in many parts of France there is as much need to preach Christianity as there is in darkest Africa" found its way into many mission articles on France.[51] American readers were told frequently that many Frenchmen had never seen a Bible and that the French people lived in a culture plagued by materialism, drunkenness, immorality, and dishonesty. Articles often trumpeted sets of statistics: 36,000 towns with no gospel witness, millions who had never seen a Bible, 80,000 spiritist healers and only 48,000 doctors, 1,446 dying every day without having heard of Christ, etc.

Occasionally articles addressed particular issues in French life which the missionaries felt necessary to bring before their constituency. For instance, French consumption of alcohol persisted as an issue aired before the American evangelical community in which many members stressed abstinence. Articles called attention to the volume of per capita alcohol consumption, the early age at which children first began to drink wine, and the related social problems. In an article published in 1954 one missionary, after noting that in France wine is carried in large tank trucks similar to those which in America were used to carry gasoline, "wondered if the excessive drinking has had the effect of deadening the consciences, so that concern for the soul is lost . . .. Our constituency in the homeland can therefore readily understand why we are anxious to get the true Gospel message, with its cleansing and saving power, to these people."[52] Other articles took up the same theme:

> Many of you no doubt read the article in
> Reader's Digest almost a year ago about alcoholism in France. Just recently This Week
> magazine, a supplement to many of your Sunday

papers, carried another article written by a
Frenchman on the same subject. Thinking
French people themselves, as well as doctors
and psychiatrists, are getting "stirred up"
about this alarming problem.

We have seen very small children in restaurants with their parents having their glasses
filled from the familiar red bottle on each
table. Wine is served freely in some student
restaurants in Paris. Alcohol is just one
force that Satan is using to numb the French
mind to the message of Power and Freedom
through Christ. Won't you join us in prayer
that the liberating power of the Holy Spirit
might touch many lives as we work to make
Christ known.[53]

The missionaries knew that alcoholism, although becoming an issue of quiet concern in some circles in
France, was a topic which would rally the emotions of
fundamental American Christians at home.

Perhaps the most frequently mentioned subjects
were those beliefs which the missionaries viewed as
rivals to evangelical Christianity. Almost every
article, brochure or book was concerned with the trust
which the French placed in Communism, Catholicism, the
occult, and materialism. The tone was often strident.
A few examples are typical:

It was the morning after a nightlong orgy of
student rioting -- one of the worst in French
history. A worker's march, 8,000 strong, had
paraded from various points around Paris.
Then three major student-groups called for a
giant demonstration in support of Communist
revolutionaries.

I walked into the courtyard of the Sorbonne,
the heart of the University of Paris. It was
not as crowded as I had expected. From an
upper window hung a red flag. A 3-foot picture of Mao Tse- Tung decorated a column.
There was no questions as to student
allegiance.[54]

*   *   *

63

In every village we seen the marks of Rome:
the cathedral spires overshadowng the house;
the statue of the Virgin or a Saint located
high upon the mountain overlooking the valley
below; fortresses, castles, and churches dat-
ing back to Roman occupation of France; a
people dwelling in spiritual darkness and cold
indifference to the message of the Word of
God.[55]

*   *   *

Since we have been in France, many of you have
written asking us to describe the French people.
In the New York Herald Tribune of June 28, 1968,
Mary Blume gave these startling statistics.

- In Paris, there is one priest for every
  5,000 inhabitants, one doctor for every
  514, and one fortune teller for every 120.

- France has 34,000 full-time astrologers
  compared to 6,000 in the United States.

- According to the French government bureau
  of statistics, more is printed on astrology
  in France each year than on astronomy,
  physics and mathematics combined.

This mysticism is indeed surprising, but it is
only the symptom of the hunger and searching
of a nation without God . . . a nation which
desperately needs God.[56]

Most of the publicity already discussed and most
of the information published about France dealt with
the need for mission work in what was seen to be a
spiritually troubled society. But the missionaries
also included in their publications accounts of the
success which they achieved in France. Missionary magazines frequently carried testimonies of French men,
women, and children in which their appreciation for
the missionary work was enthusiastically quoted:

A Paris policeman says: "My religion brought
no peace of heart. I even sought it in Communism, but almost gave up (my life) in des-
peration. Then I prayed to God to make
Himself know to me in a personal way. He

answered and brought the Light I had sought by
reading the Bible.[57]

Behind the entire publicity effort was the appeal
(sometimes implicit, sometimes explicit) for American
evangelicals to support the missionary work in France
with their prayers, their funds and above all, with
additional missionaries.

Finally, the missionary work in France came
before the public in at least two other forms. One
was the general evangelical press: articles appeared
in widely-read journals like Christianity Today, Eternity and Moody Monthly. And some of the missionaries
wrote books or booklets, the most important Let Europe
Hear, by Robert Evans.

Written information about missionary work in
France formed an important part of the entire
endeavor, although it is difficult to determine clearly the role of the printed page. The newsletters and
articles provided an important forum for the missionaries, for they enabled them periodically to put into
writing their mission and its successes and failures.
At times this was a sobering task, as the missionaries
to France wrote to their constituents about the frequent lack of response to their message and methods.
Because of the slow nature of the work in France, missionary newsletters often concerned themselves with
the amount of energy expended rather than success
achieved. Not infrequently the missionaries deluded
themselves as well as their supporters by this subtle
shift of emphasis. It was tempting to make the
prospects for the future -- "We believe we are on the
verge of a breakthrough" -- seem brighter in print
than in fact. Accurate reporting gave way to wishful
thinking, undermining the basic integrity of the communication between the missionaries and their state-
side followers. Gradually the missionary publications
showed increased sophistication in format and content.
As missionaries became more sensitive to the complex-
ities of French culture, they began to drop glib
cliches and emotional broadsides from their letters.
The expressions of virulent anti-communism and anti-
Catholicism became muted. But accurate assessment of
achievement remained rare.

It is impossible to judge the impact of missionary publicity about France on the American readers.
It is difficult to ascertain the extent to which

American evangelicals conformed their views on France to the picture portrayed by the missionaries. Pehaps the extent of successful communication can be seen in the change in the tone of missionary publicity throughout the course of the postwar period. The articles and letters from the early years were impassioned pleas for America to awaken to the spiritual needs of France, and to consider that country as a mission field, whereas later articles began to assume the acceptance of France as a mission field, and eventually reflected little novelty in the sending of missionaries to a European country.

The most direct link between the missionaries in France and American was with the mission headquarters. A few missionaries operated almost autonomously, but many others were kept on a short leash, with mission policy in France being controlled by the American office. Often the missionaires checked with the office for advice on small matters as well as large issues of policy. One prominent mission leader who had been in France for over a decade wrote to the home office to see whether he should cooperate with the touring music ensemble of a Christian college whose exact theological position was unknown to him.[58] The material communicated to the home office in the official reports revealed different emphases and areas of responsibility. Some missionary reports described in detail the spiritual discussions with French families, others wrote almost exculsively about economic matters such as automobile and building expenses, while a few informed the home office less about the work in France than about the content of the devotional period before each business meeting.

In addition to its primary functions of administration, publicity, fund raising, and tending to legal matters, the home office bore much of the responsibility for recruiting new missionaries. All missionaries in France agreed upon the need for a much larger evangelical missionary presence, yet missions were slow to develop recruitment policies and programs. One reason for this lay in the belief held by many evangelicals that it was unspiritual to recruit missionaries, or even to insist upon certain minimal standards of preparation; they thought God should be trusted to motivate potential missionaries and to equip them intellectually as well as materially. Consequently mission boards were forced to accept whomever came

along.   Sometimes poorly prepared and uncommitted
missionaries caused major problems once in France.

Gradually mission boards developed recruitment
policies and set employment standards. By the end of
the 1960's a few mission offices assigned one person
to work full-time in recruitment: touring seminaries
and Bible institutes, speaking at mission conferences,
and producing recruitment literature.   Missionary
leaders on furlough were expected to play a role in
the recruitment of new candidates. In spite of the
progress made in the recruiting process, the missionary endeavor in France remained dependent upon a small
and homogeneous applicant pool.   Increasingly,
missionary leaders in France called for an intensified
missionary education program in American churches and
evangelical schools with the aim of attracting diversified and qualified personnel. The obvious advantage
gained by encouraging missionary candidates to take
their seminary training in France was not pursued.

The relationship between the home office and the
missionaries in France was at times a positive factor
and at times a negative one.   Obviously, strong
endorsement and support from the United States
bolstered missionaries who were lagging and discouraged.   On the other hand, equally obvious, when the
missionaries felt that they were misunderstood by the
home office, or that the home office was supporting
the wrong policy in France, the frustrations and dis-
couragements of the missionary task in a strange and
unreceptive culture loomed larger than life.

Arriving in France between 1950 and 1955, the
first substantial influx of American missionaries had
been surprised and soberly impressed with the difficulty of the task in which they found themselves.
They were convinced that they had been called by God
to evangelize this nation, but they had thought little
about how this was to be done. As one missionary
arrived in France, watching from the train as the
green fields of Normandy rolled by on the ride from Le
Havre to Paris -- "just like back home" -- he bounded
from the train in the Gare St. Lazare and began passing out leaflets to the crowd on the platform. He was
very surprised to find that no one was interested.
The language barrier loomed very high for all, and for
many it was never completely surmounted. Anxious to

get on with their work, many left language school too
soon. The wives, especially if they had small children, were unable to pursue regular study, and felt
rather lost in the necessary day-to-day forays into
French society. Evangelistic methods successful in
America flopped in France. What or who, they wondered, was to blame: The method? The missionary?
The French? Cultural clash? Theological differences?
The Devil? God? Ironically, although no one claimed
to have the answer, the letters back to the States
frequently claimed that the missionaries were on the
verge of a break-through. In spite of the problems --
perhaps because of them -- new missionaries continued
to arrive.

CHAPTER III NOTES

[1]Interview with Arthur Johnston, July 19, 1972 and Robert Evans, March 6, 1973.

[2]Robert Vajko, "A History and Analysis of the Church Planting Ministry of the Evangelical Alliance Mission in France 1952-1974," Master's Thesis, Trinity Evangelical Divinity School, 1974, p. 32.

[3]Dansette, I, pp. 23, 25.

[4]For example, see Eternity, September, 1955, p. 9; Moody Monthly, October 1956, p. 4; Andre Lamorte, "Moral Sag in France," Christianity Today, June 24, 1957, p. 11.

[5]Interview with Jacques Blocher, June 15, 1973.

[6]Foreign Workers Conference summaries and notes, 1952-1970, compiled by the committees in charge of the conference; Evans, Let Europe Hear, p. 100; Jacques Ellul, lecture to Foreign Workers Conference, 1970.

[7]Kane, p. 536.

[8]David Cole, "Report on Gospel Billposting," report made to Foreign Workers Conference, 1952.

[9]Board Meeting Minutes, June 23, 1952, February 11, 1953, European Bible Institute, personal files of Robert Evans.

[10]See James Stewart, My Story (European Evangelistic Crusade, no place or date of publication given), and Eva Stuart Watt, Dynamite in Europe (London: Marshall, Morgan and Scott Ltd., 1947).

[11]Burton L. Goddard, Encyclopedia of Modern Christian Missions (Camden: Thomas Nelson & Sons, 1967), p. 559A.

[12]John D. Unruh, In the Name of Christ, p. 102; Annual Reports, 1945, 1947, Mennonite Central Committee, Akron, Pennsylvania.

[13]Guy Hershberger, The Mennonite Church in the Second World War (Scottsdale, Pennsylvania: Mennonite Publishing Company, 1951), pp. 200-203.

[14]1950 Annual Report, p. 31; 1951 Annual Report, Mennonite Central Committee, Akron, Pennsylvania.

[15]1954 Annual Report, 1957 Annual Report, p. 48, Mennonite Board of Missions, Elkhart, Indiana.

[16]The Brethren Missionary Hearld, March 1953, p. 230, National Fellowship of Brethren Churches, Winona Lake, Indiana.

[17]The Fields, July 1955, October 1963, Christian Missions in Many Lands, Spring Lake, New Jersey.

[18]Letter from John Smart, Christian Missions in Many Lands, to the author, February 15, 1973.

[19]"Missionary Calendar," n.d., Christian Missions in Many Lands, letter from Trifon Kalioudjoglou to the author, July 1973.

[20]Missionary Research Library, North American Protestant Ministries Overseas, 9th edition (Missions Advanced Research and Communication Center: Monrovia, California, 1970), p. 71.

[21]Paul H. Sheetz, The Sovereign Hand, (Wheaton, Illinois; The Evangelical Alliance Mission, 1971), p. 194.

[22]Interviews with Arthur Johnston, July 19, 1972, and Rodney Johnston, July 15, 1972; Annual Reports 1952, 1953, TEAM.

[23]1954 Annual Report, TEAM; interview with Rodney Johnston, July 15, 1972.

[24]Annual Report; Missionary Broadcaster, November 1953, p. 4; Letter from David Barnes to David Johnson, January 28, 1953, TEAM.

[25]1954 Annual Report, TEAM.

[26]Interview with Jesberg, December 14, 1972.

[27] _Missionary Broadcaster_, March 1957, TEAM, p. 10.

[28] _Missionary Broadcaster_, June 1955, TEAM, p. 6; interviews with Arthur Johnston, July 19, 1972, and Rodney Johnston, July 15, 1972.

[30] Rodney Johnston, newsletter, October 1955, TEAM.

[31] Interview with Arthur Johnston, June 13, 1973; letter from Arthur Johnston to David Johnson, January 6, 1956, TEAM.

[32] 1968 Annual Conference Report, TEAM, p. 42.

[33] Field Conference Minutes, June 2-8, 1959, TEAM, p. 13.

[34] Interviews with John Stauffacher, Baptist Mid-Missions, June 12, 1972, and with Carol Wilson, TEAM, June 20, 1973.

[35] Roland Allen, _Missionary Methods: St. Pauls or Ours?_ (Grand Rapids: William B. Eerdmans Publishing Company, 1962) p. 49.

[36] Letter from Vernon Mortenson, general director of TEAM, to Louise Lazaro, April 22, 1966. TEAM.

[37] Treasurers' reports in the Annual Conference Reports, 1953-1968, TEAM.

[38] Letter from Nelson Bezanson, administrative assistant, TEAM, to the author, March 16, 1974.

[39] Annual Reports, 1953-1970, Greater Europe Mission.

[40] Robert Evans, paper read to conference of the Greater Europe Mission, October 10, 1966, p. 3.

[41] Latourette, _Missions and the American Mind_, p. 34.

[42] These brief quotations, representative of many similar ones, are taken from an early European Bible Institute _News Bulletin_, 1952, personal files of Robert Evans.

[43]Field Conference Minutes, June 2-8, 1959, TEAM, p. 13.

[44]Arthur Johnston, newsletter, August 24, 1960, TEAM.

[45]Newsletters, 1969, TEAM.

[46]Enid Skuce, newsletter, April 8, 1969, Unevangelized Fields Mission (UFM), Bala-Cynwyd, Pennsylvania.

[47]Naomi Umenhofer, newsletter, April 1969, UFM.

[48]Notes taken at a missionary conference sent to the author by Joy Copp, former TEAM missionary, March, 1974.

[49]Missionary Broadcaster, May, 1953, TEAM, p. 8.

[50]Herald, November 3, 1951, National Fellowship of Brethren Churches, Winona Lake, Indiana, p. 745.

[51]Usually cited from Life World Library: France, (New York: Time, Inc., 1961), p. 117.

[52]Missionary Broadcaster, February, 1954, TEAM, pp. 3, 8.

[53]Rodney Johnston, newsletter, October 1955, TEAM.

[54]Walther Olsen, "Is Paris Burning?", Impact, Summer 1968, Conservative Baptist Foreign Mission Society (CBFMS), Wheaton, Illinois.

[55]Missionary Brochures, UFM, n.d.

[56]Youth For Christ, Wheaton, Illinois, newsletter, September 1968.

[57]"France", brochure, late 1950's, TEAM.

[58]Letter, Arthur Johnston to Vernon Mortenson, September 23, 1964, TEAM.

CHAPTER IV

THE SEARCH FOR STRATEGY 1955 - 1965

In the late 1950's and in the 1960's France experienced political, social, and economic changes which were revolutionary. A troubled, stagnant society became mobile and affluent, though no less troubled. The American missionaries, experiencing enough difficulty in understanding traditional French culture, faced the additional problem of adapting to a society in rapid transition.

The political changes were initially more obvious. For more than a decade the Fourth Republic demonstrated that it was incapable of providing effective government for France. Criticized and disdained, the weak parliamentary regime could not survive the national crisis caused by colonial conflict. In 1954 the French army suffered a humiliating withdrawal from Indochina. Then, having just lost their empire in Southeast Asia, the French were confronted by another protracted colonial war in Algeria. By the spring of 1958 the French nation was bitterly divided by the Algerian question. Unable to find a solution to the military and political dilemma, and even powerless to control its own army, the Fourth Republic gave way to the emergency government of General Charles de Gaulle, and then to the authoritarian Fifth Republic. Under de Gaulle's forceful presidency, France extricated itself from the Algerian war, and embarked upon the Gaullist foreign policy which stressed independence and grandeur. The French government withdrew its military participation in NATO, and de Gaulle ordered American troops to leave France. The development of a costly nuclear strike force and the attempt to dominate the Common Market manifested de Gaulle's quest for French leadership in Europe.

However, the striking political and diplomatic changes did not affect the American missionaries or the French people as much as did the new social and economic trends. The postwar economic recovery which had languished in the early 1950's shifted into high gear in the 1960's. Swarms of new automobiles choked French cities, clusters of stark concrete apartment buildings sprang up in suburban fields, television captured domestic life. The French became preoccupied with planning their leisure time. They lived for their summer vacations and le weekend. The ancient

73

cultural and spiritual values of France were being supplanted by the materialist aspirations of a modern consumer society. Already thoroughly secularized, increasingly de-Christianized, the new France showed even less interest in religion.

Notwithstanding these trends, the tempo of American mission activity in France accelerated sharply in the decade between 1955 and 1965. This period was initially highlighted by the efforts in mass evangelism by the American evangelist Billy Graham. More important, the leading missions solidified their purpose and adopted a clearly defined strategy for missionary work in France. Failure, however, claimed more of the story than success. Although the total number of missionaries in France continued to climb (there were at least 145 by 1965), a number of Americans who went to France in the first wave of the early 1950's became discouraged, and returned to the United States.

By the time of his 1955 campaign in Paris, Billy Graham had become internationally known. After the conclusion of his highly successful London campaign in 1954, Graham spoke in Paris to a group of 2,700 Protestant pastors and their assistants. The audience, representing the entire theological spectrum of French Protestantism, was frankly curious about this man who had preached to millions. Although many did not share Graham's evangelical views, the reception given his remarks on evangelism was, in the words of one reporter, "one of quiet, conservative enthusiasm."[1]

The direct result of the 1954 visit by Graham was a move by certain French pastors to invite him to Paris for an evangelistic crusade. There were significant obstacles to overcome, not the least of which was the tarnished image given to mass evangelistic campaigns by some of the haphazard American efforts of the immediate postwar years. However, impressed by the careful planning and organization of the Billy Graham Evangelistic Association, the French clergy gradually began to lose their reserve.[2] American evangelical missionaries did much of the advance work for planning the crusade, organizing the counselors, and forming the choir. The Americans acquired insight into French culture and the French way of doing things, while the French pastors, accustomed to separate and often highly individualistic ministries, found that much could be accomplished through teamwork.

74

Beginning on June 5, 1955, the first Billy Graham Crusade in Paris met for five nights in the Velodrome d'Hiver, the largest auditorium in Paris. Surpassing all expectations, attendance averaged nearly 8,000 per night, and signed decision cards numbered 2,200, a percentage of response three times higher than the highly successful meetings just held in London and Glasgow.[3] The 1955 Billy Graham campaign was the first project in which most of the American missionaries and the French evangelicals were partners, and the new cooperation between the two groups was perhaps the campaign's most important result. However, the campaign's large evangelistic goal remained unfulfilled. Many of those who signed a decision card declined to show further interest. The French evangelical community was not visibly enlarged by the Billy Graham campaign. Nonetheless the American missionaries applauded the temporary unity among evangelicals, both French and American, and the encouraging attendance figures.

Eight years later, in 1963, Graham conducted a more extensive French campaign, with meetings not only in Paris, but also in Lyon, Toulouse, and Mulhouse. In addition to the 60,000 who attended, many more viewed portions on television. The results in terms of cooperation and encouragement within the Franco-American evangelical community continued the momentum initiated by the 1955 campaign. In a major American religious periodical, a French evangelical leader, noting that the campaign attendance equaled or surpassed the normal Sunday Protestant church attendance throughout all of France, concluded that the campaign showed the interest of the French public, not just the churchgoer, in hearing the American evangelist.[4] However, successful evangelistic campaigns required the support of the local clergy, both before and after the evangelist's efforts. The evangelical enthusiasm over, the Graham campaigns could not overcome the continued reserve of many Reformed church leaders. The American evangelist's stress upon immediate and emotional personal commitment ran counter to the normal French Reformed emphasis upon the path of baptism, confirmation and gradual instruction. The inability of mass evangelism to integrate its converts into the evangelical churches made it obvious that it was at best an accessory to the missionary enterprise. Some other strategy had to be found if the American missionaries were to make an impact upon religion in France.

After a one-year furlough in the United States, Arthur Johnston of the Evangelical Alliance Mission (TEAM), returned to France in 1956 to find that the youth work which he painstakingly had built up in his first three years in France had disintegrated completely in his absence. Of the group of thirty-five young people, only one had retained any interest. Furthermore, there had been almost no success in reaching adults. With the exception of a handful in Vitry and a small youth club for Americans living in Paris, TEAM had nothing to show for its first four years in France. Johnston realized that youth work alone produced no lasting results in France. It was obvious that a new strategy had to be devised.

TEAM's youth work suffered from the mission's inability or unwillingness to establish a relationship with local French churches. Theological differences and presumptions as well as cultural barriers divided the French and the Americans. The personal background and religious education of the American evangelical missionaries predisposed them to regard the Roman Catholic churches as unacceptable. Johnston came to a similar conclusion about the Reformed church in France. Consequently he decided that the Americans needed to start French evangelical churches from scratch. Under Johnston's leadership the TEAM missionaries in France formally adopted a plan which focused their energies toward the organization and establishment of entirely new churches. The failure of the youth work was the initial impetus for the decision, and it was supported by Johnston's view of French Protestantism which led him to conclude that "historically ingrown French Protestantism, blinded by false ecumenism, had failed to reach the masses with the Gospel."[5] Although acknowledging the "small, faithful and helpful nucleus" of French evangelicals, Johnston was convinced of the apostasy of most of French Protestantism, and determined to start a new denomination.[6]

By dismissing out-of-hand the people and respected heritage of the Reformed church, the missionaries took a step which limited severely their impact on French society. In the following two decades most American missions in France would follow TEAM's critical and even fateful decision. There were at least two areas of common ground on which the evangelical missionaries and the Reformed church might have met. First, they were both part of a very small Protestant minority in a traditionally Catholic country. But the influence and respect commanded by Protestants in French society was far greater than their numbers might indicate. The missionaries' decision to disassociate themselves from these fellow Protestants in France denied themselves a possible solution to their problem of identity. Second, and far more important, the missionaries and the French evangelicals alike agreed that there were 50,000 to 60,000 evangelical Christians scattered throughout Reformed congregations in France. This figure amounted to about one-half of the entire evangelical population of France. Amazingly, the missionaries made almost no attempt to contact these people. Furthermore, the missionaries generally did not even attempt to reap the benefits which might have been obtained from locating their work in the regions of France which were historically Protestant. A map of Protestant strongholds and one of missionary activity show very little overlap.[7]

The reasons for the missionary predisposition against the Reformed church lay more in their American background than in the actual situation in France. Almost all the missionaries came from independent or Baptist churches and schools which had been founded in the early twentieth century in reaction to the increasingly liberal theological orientation of mainline American denominations. The missionaries were automatically distrustful of any large denomination or ecclesiastical organization, especially those like the French Reformed churches, which were associated with the World Council of Churches and the ecumenical movement. The question of ignoring the French Reformed church provoked little debate in most large American mission agencies because their major interest and experience lay, not in France, but in the underdeveloped non-Christian nations of the third world where there was no established church. Most missionaries simply discounted the Reformed church even before they arrived in France. Consequently a majority of them never once attended the local Reformed church.

For its part, the Reformed church did little to welcome the missionaries. In addition to the wide theological difference between most Reformed pastors and the missionaries, there was also a jurisdictional problem. Since the Reformed church had divided all of France into parishes, the missionaries inevitably operated within the baliwick of a pastor of a Reformed church. Often the French pastors felt that tradition and etiquette required the missionaries to ask permission before beginning their work, although there was no legal obligation to do so.

The strange lack of contact between the American Protestant missionaries and the largest Protestant church in France cried out for explanation. One evangelical missions authority examined the cool relationship between the missionaries and the existing Protestant churches in France (and perhaps attempted to justify it) by comparing it to the situation faced by Protestant missionaries who first went to the Middle East in the early nineteenth century. It had been their intention to revive the Eastern churches and through them evangelize the Muslim population. "The attempt was not very successful because the Orthodox churches did not wish to be revived and resented any attempt on the part of the western missionaries to infiltrate their ranks. Something of the same situation exists in the churches of Europe. It has not proved easy to cooperate with them for reasons which are both theological and cultural."[9]

Among the cultural barriers, the Americans pointed to the class difference between the normally more affluent Reformed congregations and the missionaries.[10] But there was no evidence of any specific problems stemming from class difference, and this issue may have been based more on myth than substance. Another problem was one of numbers. The missionaries were convinced that many Reformed pastors viewed the creation of another Protestant work in their community as a competitor, not an ally. The French Reformed pastors feared that some sheep would be stolen from their already tiny flocks.[11]

Although the story was not one of complete non-cooperation (here and there a few missionaries developed close working relationships with evangelical Reformed pastors) most missionaries decided that their initial suspicions about the Reformed church were confirmed by their experience in France. The missionaries felt that cooperative efforts were fruitless because of the Reformed church's reluctance to see the need for aggressive evangelism, and because the missionaries doubted that converts from their own evangelistic effort would not receive the necessary Biblical teaching as members of Reformed congregations. Mission paternalism, however benignly conceived, played a strong role. New converts usually appeared shaky to the missionaries, so their religious environment was controlled carefully. Missions with strict policies, like TEAM, made a special effort to avoid contact with the Reformed church because mission leaders feared that cooperation with liberal churches would serve only to confuse TEAM's converts. In some cases the differences between the local Reformed pastor and the missionaries became so large that the missionaries claimed to have had their work publicly and privately opposed by the pastor.

Striking out on his own, then, Johnston led TEAM down the road to a new French denomination sponsored by the American missionaries. His decision found additional support in the Chicago headquarters of TEAM where Vernon Mortenson, though not yet general director, had been changing slowly the general emphasis of TEAM's worldwide ambitions toward church planting. Although not a revolutionary concept in the 1950's, church planting was not the widely accepted missionary strategy which it would become in the 1970's. Many missions in France and elsewhere around the world took little care to formulate any strategy at all, other than "sowing the seed" or "general mission work", whatever that might mean. TEAM's decision to devote itself to the formidable yet delicate task of planting new churches in a de-Christianized culture which still contained a tiny indigenous evangelical church committed the mission to an uncharted course. TEAM's accomplishments and mistakes were bound to influence other American missions in France. In opting for the strategy of starting new churches (rather than forming relationships with existing churches) TEAM and other missions to follow were influenced more by the cleavages in American Protestantism and by general evangelical missionary strategy in the third world than by careful analysis of the unique situation in France.

Adopted in 1956, TEAM's A Guide Plan for France was a detailed, if somewhat overly optimistic document. An important part of the plan was the decision to concentrate the work in the southern suburbs of Paris. Although the mission toyed with the idea of scattering its missionaries in cities across France, TEAM decided to concentrate in one region where missionaries (and later churches) could be of help to each other. After some study they concluded that the northern suburbs were too heavily communist to expect much success; the western suburbs with their upper middle class flavor were anticipated to be unreceptive to mission work; the eastern suburbs had at least one evangelical center at the institute in Nogent; and the southern suburbs, devoid of independent evangelical churches, were rapidly growing with an influx of lower middle class people with whom the missionaries felt socially comfortable. The missionaries realized that France was becoming urbanized rapidly, and they hoped that evangelism might reap greater success among those who flocked to the cities, leaving their rural roots and inhibitions behind. Calling for the establishment of at least four churches in the first year, a Bible school or seminary within three years, and complete transfer of the work to French Christians within the work within five years, the Guide Plan would bear little resemblance to the reality of tortuously slow progress.

The first church established by TEAM in France grew out of the work in Vitry. Since 1953, when several missionaries first moved to that city, a small group had been put together, starting first with children's classes, then with their parents and other adults contacted by the Americans. Progress was slow because parents and neighbors were at first suspicious of the missionaries' intentions. The missionaries found it difficult to meet people, and almost impossible to get to know them. They were accustomed to the wide-open American culture where neighbors became friends quickly and borrowed each other's lawn mowers. Friendships took much longer to build in France. Families living on the same street could remain lifelong strangers. The closed nature of French society and the vigilantly guarded privacy of the French home were sources of frequent rebuff and consequent discouragement. The closely-knit nuclear family unit usually did not lead to the conversion of large extended families which was a key factor in missionary success in other lands. But by 1957, in addition to three meetings per week for children and teens, a group of about twenty met regularly on Sunday afternoons in the home of one of the missionaries. It was not a group of "ordinary" Frenchmen. Sunday worship, so normal to the missionaries, loomed as a major change in normal French social patterns. Since Sunday afternoon was the time most French families spent

together at home, those who attended the Vitry meetings usually were individuals with no family in the
vicinity or who lacked strong family ties. Their
attendance at the Sunday afternoon service was not the
sacrifice it would have been for typical French
families accustomed to a three hour Sunday dinner and
afternoon promenade.[12] The first TEAM church,
like many missionary churches to follow, depended upon
parishioners from the margin of French society.

Growing too large to continue to meet in a home,
the group was led by the missionaries to the point
where it decided to purchase a building. Borrowing
money from the headquareters in the United States, the
small number of recent converts to evangelical Christianity purchased a former shoe factory on Vitry's
Avenue André Maginot which they and the missionaries
renovated as a chapel. The missionaries plastered and
painted, while an American army chaplain furnished the
salle évangélique with a pulpit and chairs. The
establishment of the new evangelical church in Vitry,
officially inaugurated on May 17, 1959, was welcomed
by French evangelicals, and even received acclaim from
the two pastors of the Reformed churches in neighboring towns.[13]

A church was organized, a building purchased, but
the expected growth failed to materialize. Although a
Sunday morning service and a Sunday school were inaugurated, the membership remained at about twenty. The
primary reason for this, the missionaries concluded
only much later, was the social and political climate
of the area in which the church was located. The missionaries had not been wise to concentrate their work
in working class Vitry. In the staunchly communist
city anyone (but especially men) ran the risk of
incurring the scorn and even rebuke of his neighbors
if he attended a church, particularly one in which
Americans were involved. The resistant social
environment was one of the problems resulting from
having the area of work determined by the missionaries' place of residence, instead of the other way
around. The American missionaries had successfully
established a church, and had achieved the higher goal
of turning it over to a French leader whom they had
trained. But the church in Vitry was destined to be
perennially small, debt-ridden, and without much
impact.

The experience in Vitry illustrated the problems posed to the missionaries by the French class structure. French evangelicals normally worked along horizontal planes within social classes. The Americans, initially ignorant of the intricacies of French society, attempted to bring together people from different classes. As a foreigner the missionary could move between classes more readily than could a Frenchman, but sooner or later uneasiness or squabbles between the classes in the group would erupt, and the missionary would be perplexed by the group's disintegration.[14] French social structure provoked a sustained debate among the missionaries on the question of whether their groups and churches should be socially homogeneous or heterogeneous. Some were convinced that the groups they were attempting to organize should be socially diverse because the churches of the New Testatment era included aristocrats, merchants, and slaves.[15] Others, citing statistics from church growth studies in the twentieth century, stressed that social homogeneity was the key to growth.[16] The missionaries did not adhere rigorously to any strategy concerning social class, although they usually worked among the lower middle class. They were ill at ease with the working class, and rarely could afford to live among the bourgeoisie. And they made almost no penetration of the upper class, nor of the community or national leadership.

While the first attempt of TEAM to establish a church, that at Vitry, might be termed at best a marginal success, the second attempt, at Orly, was viewed by many observers as the most significant achievement of American missionaries in France. Its story provides an appropriate case study of church planting.

It began on the way home from a family picnic. In July 1956, Arthur and Rodney Johnston, their wives and six children were piled in an old Citroen. They stopped at a railway crossing in Orly, a growing city six miles south of Paris, and known internationally for its airport. Johnston noticed a scrawled sign in a window announcing an evangelical meeting in a tent. After the train passed, he drove across the tracks, parked the car, and walked back. Knocking on the door of the house, Johnston was received by an elderly woman named Dufour, and he introduced himself as a pastor. She immediately invited him to speak to the little group that evening. Later she told Johnston that she had been praying for seven years that someone would come to Orly to teach the small group of women about the Bible. Meeting regularly with Johnston on Saturday evenings for a Bible study in the Dufour kitchen, the group of two or three women was the genesis of the Orly church. The membership of the group slowly multiplied. In 1956 there were only two or three, the next year four or six, then ten, twenty, forty until in 1956 there were one hundred. The group officially organized itself as l'église évangélique d'Orly, and decided to purchase land on which to erect a church building. They finally selected a building lot surrounded by a growing apartment development on the Avenue des Martyrs de Chateaubriand, a main road connecting Orly with Paris. But they found that the building fund which they had started was inadequate. Although the TEAM headquarters offered a $5,000 loan and a $2,500 matching grant toward the purchase price of $12,000, it was obvious to the group that the funds could be raised only by their heavy donations. Cutting deeply into their resources (one woman had no money left to buy winter coal) the group raised the necessary amount. The property was finally purchased in early 1961.

As the church matured, the missionaries assured mission control over church policies. Arthur Johnston was convinced that the missionaries in France had a strong moral obligation to the churches in the United States that supported his effort. American evangelical tradition and practice molded the image of the new churches in France. Johnston was particularly concerned that the orthodox evangelical theology with which the young churches were formed should not be lost. Accordingly the requirements for membership in TEAM's churches were stringent, including (in addition to the basic evangelical statement of faith) pledges to abide by strict standards of behavior. While assuring a committed membership which was compatible with mission philosophy, the stress on accountability to home churches led others to criticize TEAM for imparting American cultural forms in addition to its basic evangelical message.

The next step, the construction of a church building, combined the dedication of the new French believers with financial support channeled through the TEAM Chicago office. The church building at Orly, of unusual and striking contemporary design, meant more to the TEAM missionaries than a shelter from the elements. The building demonstrated that the mission was not a store-front or a fly-by-night organization, but rather that it was serieux and had a visage. This was a major change in the attitude with which TEAM had originally come to France. For the first few years, expecting to accomplish the evangelization of France rapidly, the Chicago office of TEAM did not wish to encumber the mission in France with real estate.[17] By the 1960's, the pace and aspirations more in step with French reality, TEAM was doing all it could to appear established. The building helped, although the financial burden was large.

The TEAM church planting effort expanded steadily to other southern Paris suburbs: Orsay, Fresnes, Créteil, Chilly-Mazarin. The Orsay church never grew large enough to initiate a building campaign, so they decided to make a church out of the garage attached to the misson headquarters. It was not uncommon for missionary churches to get their start in a garage; several remained there.

The TEAM church at Fresnes, three miles west of Orly, grew out of a small home Bible study, and was largely the result of the efforts of missionary Ivan Peterson. The Petersons first came to France in 1962 after being forced to abandon their missionary careers in the former Belgian Congo. The experienced missionary couple spent a long time adapting to the change from Africa to France, and became discouraged: "After crowds of thousands in the Congo and hundreds in our revival meetings in American, we need patience with the small groups in France." While many missionaries labored under the conviction that it took as much work to reach one Frenchman as ten Americans, Peterson compared one Frenchman to one hundred Congolese.[18]

After the small Bible study had grown to a group of twelve, the TEAM missionaries decided that the Fresnes church should be formally organized in December 1965. A series of evangelistic campaigns helped to increase the numbers. Peterson's brand of evangelism was agressive and American. His practice of concluding each service with an invitation to make a public conversion, while shared by other TEAM preachers, was not common in France. In 1966, with attendance averaging thirty-five, the energetic pastor led the church to purchase a parcel of land on Avenue Jean Pierre, near the center of Fresnes. A costly church building of contemporary architectural design was erected in 1971, and officially dedicated the following year. By 1975 membershp was forty-five, with average Sunday attendance slightly larger.

TEAM's original focus on French youth was not forgotten in the course of its commitment to church planting. The camp ministry became the primary arm of the youth work, and the missionaries soon had more applications than vacancies for the Easter, Christmas and summer camps. Taking the name Jeunesse Ardente for the movement, Rodney Johnston urged the mission to purchase an old hotel at Praz-de-Lys (Haute Savoie).[19] The old wooden building, functional but in need of considerable repair, clung to a remote Alpine plateau, nestled under the surrounding peaks. Youth work, the original ambition of the Johnston brothers, and the area of great failure in the mid-1950's, was once again part of TEAM's program by 1965.

All the work of TEAM in France was coordinated by the formation of the Alliance des Eglises Evangéliques Indépendantes (AEEI). Shortly after the decision to commit TEAM to church planting, the mission decided that the legal aspects of this plan could best be handled by the formation of a French religious association, (association cultuelle). Membership in the Alliance included prominent French evangelicals as well as the American missionaries from TEAM. The Alliance sought to give cohesion to what was hoped to be a growing number of TEAM churches, and it also intended to tie the TEAM effort more closely to the French community. But although the number of French members of the Alliance grew continually, the Americans were careful to retain legal control of the organization.[20]

In the 1960's a growing number of American missions followed TEAM's decision to concentrate upon planting new churches. The Greater Europe Mission, the agency which sponsored the European Bible Institute, began a church planting effort in several cities in northern France. Their church planting attempt began without the rigid doctrinal framework which marked the TEAM effort. They agreed upon a basic evangelical statement of faith to which converts in churches were expected to subscribe, but in other areas such as the mode of baptism and the future affiliation of the church (topics which were tightly regimented in TEAM's plan) there was latitude.[21]

The difference between these two positions would highlight the story of the establishment of new churches by Americans in postwar France. Some missions felt that their assemblies should be committed to a highly specific code of belief and conduct, even if this meant that numbers remained small. Others were hopeful that flexibility on issues of secondary importance would make it easier for Frenchmen to embrace evangelical Christianity. Behind this debate lay the fundamental question underlying the entire mission to France: to what extent, according to the missionaries, did a commitment to evangelical Christianity require a break with French cultural norms? Throughout the first generation of American missionary work in postwar France there was continuing controversy about this most basic issue.

The church planting attempt of the Greater Europe Mission never achieved much. Several missionaries and several years of effort in small northern industrial cities near Lille produced no evangelical group, while in Amiens the little church group which missionary Ronald Hoyle finally knit together was composed more of transfers from other churches than from new converts. With substantial aid from American donors and volunteer workers, they Amiens group purchased a former movie theater which they renovated as a small chapel. The missionary continued to serve as pastor.

A few other American missions attempted to start new churches in France in the late 1950's and early 1960's. Baptist Mid-Missions personnel labored in Parisian suburbs (Savigny-sur-Orge and Ris-Orangis) and Bordeaux. The Bible Christian Union plodded on in several cities in the Loire Valley: Tours, Vendome, Blois, and Romorantin. Not inclined to mull over strategy options, the missionaries were wedded to traditional methods (children's classes, street preaching, tent meetings, etc.), and achieved only small success.

The Americans were so anxious to get a church started, and so proud of their achievement once a tiny church was organized, that they failed to realize that their small success made greater success less likely. The evangelical missionaries came from a culture which accepted and even took pride in small independent churches. Many midwestern towns supported a different church on each street corner. The French saw things differently. For them, there was only one church, or perhaps two in regions where Protestants were visible. Everything else was a sect. They lumped together all little religious groups, no matter how divergent their beliefs: Adventists, Jehovah's Witnesses, Friends of Man, Mennonites, Brethren, Baptists, Salvation Army, Pentecostals, Christian Scientists, etc.[22] In American history small dissenting sects had grown into major denominations. While not all sects became large churches, most large churches had started as sects. In France, the relationship between sect and church was antithetical, not evolutionary. Sects remained outside the center of traditional French religious culture, and so did the sectarian missionary churches.[23] Nonetheless in the late 1950's and early 1960's the search for strategy took most American missions in France to the policy of establishing small indigenous churches.

The missionaries of the Grace Brethren started down this path, but branched off on a different course. Working by himself in Lyon, Fred Fogle, one of the early missionaries to France, attempted to organize a small church in the 1950's. Fogle built up a small group of believers by door-to-door visitation, a summer camp which he organized and directed himself, and by a portable hall project. He had constructed a readily assembled and disassembled hall with a capacity of eighty which he hauled to sites all over Lyon for film showings and evangelistic messages. He was able to organize a store-front preaching center to which twenty or thirty people came on Sunday mornings. But the group had weaknesses related to its small size. Only ten of the members were men, and there was little inclination toward leadership among the parishioners. The small congregation had not made an impact on its own city.[24] The lack of French leadership in the group became an acute problem at the time when the Fogles planned to return to the United States for a one-year furlough in 1960. Although it had been the intention of the mission to establish a Brethren Church adhering to mission principles, the missionaries decided that the group's chances for survival were slim, and therefore the Free Church (Eglise Libre), a small French evangelical denomination, was asked to assume control of it. The 1964 merger allowed the missionary-founded group to survive as part of the Lyon Eglise Libre congregation which grew so rapidly that it soon needed a larger building.

Although Fogle had established a small evangelical group, the midwesterner's conclusions amounted to something less than an endorsement of the church planting strategy which was being adopted by most missions. He began to perceive the crippling frustration if not the complete futility of the strategy of each mission establishing its own little churches. Fogle was bothered by the weaknesses in the group, especially the inclination of the French to let the American missionary assume all the responsibility of leadership. This, coupled with the dramatic growth which the group shared under the auspices of the Eglise Libre after Fogle left, convinced him that American missonaries could make a more positive contribution to the evangelization of France by remaining in the background, instructing and prodding the French evangelicals. He later took a position on the faculty of the European Bible Institute.

It became increasingly common for American missionaries in France to change the nature of their work and even their mission affiliation. Teachers would become church planters, church planters would become teachers, street evangelists would go into radio work. The changes sometimes reflected the missionaries' clearer perception of how they might be more effective in French society. But more often it was discouragement, not perception, which prompted an abrupt change in activity. A number of missionaries were moved by the furtive hope that change alone would turn failure into success.

Other problems could cut short missionary service. Missionary work in France proved to be a strain for the missionaries, and missionary life was a strain for their families. Parents could be cruelly torn between their commitments to their work and to their children. They sometimes felt guilty for career decisions which forced their children to cope with a foreign culture. Most missionary parents claimed it was necessary to maintain an American home, not only for the general purpose of giving the children the benefit of a bicultural background, but also for the specific purpose of maintaining their contact with the American evangelical traditions and community.

Cultural adaptation could make child rearing more demanding. Most missionary wives found their days filled with the tasks of child rearing and housekeeping, but some also carried additional duties of

teaching child evangelism classes and Sunday School,
women's groups, and personal evangelistic responsibilities. The missionary wives, like, for instance, the
wives of American businessmen in Europe, usually felt
the cultural and linguistic isolation more deeply than
did their husbands. But while the businessman's wife
might complain of boredom in the strange environment,
the missionary wife's responsibilities led more often
to extreme fatigue and even emotional breakdown than
to boredom.[25]   While the missionaries never confessed that an American wife was a handicap, the
several missionaries who married French women claimed
a smoother and more successful cultural adaptation.

Children, the missionaries found, opened many
French doors to American families, but the problem
which adaptation to French culture presented to missionary children caused concern, anguish, and even the
termination of some missionary careers. While younger
children could adapt quite easily to their new environment, school age youngsters often experienced
severe social and emotional trials. A few missionaries admitted that the personalities of their older
children remained scarred by the trauma of immersion
into a new and often unsympathetic culture. Many
parents were tormented by the doubts about their mission in France which stemmed from the nightly sobbing
of homesick children.[26]

Most missionary children eventually bridged the
cultural gap, attended French schools, and some even
excelled. But others found the academic and social
pressures of French education to be too great. A few
of these enrolled in the American school on the west
side of Paris, but financial and transporation difficulties eliminated this option for most missionary
families. In the late 1960's several missions joined
in a feasibility study about a cooperative school for
missionary children, although no concrete action on
this project was taken.[27]   The other alternative
was to return to the United States, a step taken by a
number of missionaries, some of whom had been engaged
in relatively successful work.

Another Grace Brethren missionary, Thomas Julien
found himself drifting over to the position adopted by
the Catholic H. Godin in his influential La France:
Pays de Mission.[28]   Godin's startling conclusions
portrayed France as a neo-pagan society to which even
the Catholic church had a missionary obligation. But

the large gap between the French and Christianity was not being bridged by the institutional church. Catholic attempts to solve this problem included the abortive worker-priest movement of the early 1950's.[29] Julien realized that the American missionaries' efforts were frustrated by the large gap between the French people and the institutional church. An even larger gap separated French culture and American evangelical Christianity. What was needed, he decided, was a "neutral" bridge to bring the two together. Accordingly, in 1965 the mission purchased a fourteenth-century chateau in the village of Saint-Albain, ten miles north of Macon, and about one hour's drive north of Lyon. An imposing stone structure atop a hill above the small village, the chateau commanded a view of the fertile fields of the Saonne valley and the hills in the distance. For the rest of the decade the Grace Brethren strategy was to attract French people, mainly youth, to the variety of programs offered at the chateau. The mission affirmed that its basic goal, the establishment of French churches, had not changed, but the means to achieve that end had been altered to place the missionaries in supporting, rather than front line positions.[30]

The Mennonite work in France, begun as postwar relief work conducted by the Mennonite Central Committee, had fallen under the control of the Mennonite Board of Missions and Charities, which organized a small church in the southern suburbs of Paris. In 1956 Robert Witmer, a newly arrived Canadian missionary, assumed control of the small congregation. Under his leadership the group expanded and forged a close relationship between American and French Mennonites. Furthermore, the mission won acclaim for its pace-setting program for retarded children. In 1961 the Mennonites opened the first workshop in the Paris area for adolescent retarded children. French families with retarded children faced a critical problem when the child grew beyond school age. Working parents of retarded adolescents did not know what to do with teens who possessed energy and certain ability, but who could not function in a normal job nor be left home without supervision. The Mennonite Sheltered Workshop provided an answer for as many as forty-eight families. The youngsters performed simple operations such as assembling zippers, cleaning and reassembling air passenger headsets, or filing rough edges off of machine parts. They were able to work at their own pace without the tensions of a competitive world too fast for them. At the end of each month they had the reward of a pay envelope. In 1965 the mission purchased the lot next door, straining its resources, and constructed a larger workshop. By this time the workshop had won not only the acclaim of the French government but also its financial support. In 1967 the mission and the French Mennonites opened another center for sixty retarded young men in Hautefeuille, about twenty-five miles from Paris. French national television devoted a documentary program to the Mennonite assistance to retarded youth.[31]

The Mennonite mission in Chatenay-Malabry, Foyer Fraternel, occupied a unique place in the story of American missionary activity in France. First, the Mennonite mission combined evangelism and church planting with significant social work. Second, they avoided problems with French evangelicals by making clear their desire to assist the French Mennonites rather than to compete with them. Their relationship with the French Mennonites was much closer and more productive than, for instance, that of the American Baptist missionaries with the French Baptists. Third, while many American missions were criticized for their sectarian principles, the Mennonites, though maintaining evangelical beliefs, were able to establish cooperation with many groups and agencies. They were involved in several cooperative projects with other missions, and in their workshops for the retarded they established a relationship with the French state. No other mission did this. The Mennonite work in France emphasized their world-wide reputation for compassion and cooperation.

Of the American missions which began to work in France in the 1950's, the most distinctive in terms of origin and the area of activity was the Alpine Mission to France. This organization evolved from a small British mission which had conducted evangelistic work in the 1930's in the Haute Savoie between Mont Blanc and the Swiss frontier. After World War II it was difficult to raise money in Britain, so an American group assumed responsibility for the mission.[32] Its first American missionary, Jane Bernardo, had just seen her plans to become a missionary to India fall through when mission leader Donald Orr spoke at her church in Rhode Island and convinced her about the need for missionaries in France. Arriving in France in 1952, she found the first years to be lonely and discouraging, as she lived by herself in a windowless

91

room above a cheese shop in Albertville, struggling
with the French language. Culture shock was a problem
for all the missonaries, but was less of an ordeal for
the missionaries who went to the Paris region than for
a single young woman who was dismayed by the squalor,
suspicions, and primitive living conditions of an isolated mountain village.[33] The summer evangelistic
work in which Bernardo and the Orrs busied themselves
was unique. Their aim was to evangelize the tiny
mountain villages strung along the remote narrow green
valleys which twisted up to the rocky and snow-capped
peaks. Arriving at a village at dusk, Orr would set a
slide screen on the roof of his old car, borrow electricity from the rustic cafe, and show slides and give
a talk on the life of Christ. After giving an invitation to make a personal commitment to Chirst, the missionaries would move on. It was not a rewarding
ministry. Rural France had always been infertile
ground for itinerant evangelism.[34] The villagers
were suspicious and often hostile. Although the Orrs
saw few, if any results from this work, they and the
young American girl persisted year after year, village
after village, in the Alpine valleys of France.

By 1961 the Alpine Mission to France was having
problems in the United States because the administrative work was done on a volunteer basis by men who
were already too busy. A more regularized office pro-
cedure was necessary, but the small mission could not
afford to support an American business office. At
about the same time, the Unevangelized Fields Mission
(headquarters in a Main Line suburb of Philadelphia),
a large interdenominational mission with missionaries
mainly in Africa and Asia, was considering expansion
of its work to Europe. It was hesitant to do so with
its name which its leaders feared might offend
European sensitivities. The needs of both missions
were met by a merger which was accomplished in
February 1962. The Alpine Mission became part of the
Unevangelized Fields Mission, although the former name
was retained for use in France.

Of all the mission agencies working in France,
only one was attached to a major American denomination. The Southern Baptist Convention's Foreign
Mission Board, largest of all North American mission
boards, sent personnel to France in response to an
invitation from the French. In 1957 Baptists among
the American military forces in France founded an
English-language Baptist Church in Saran, a suburb of

Orleans. After preaching there in 1959, pastor Henri
Vincent, president of the French Baptist Federation,
wrote to the Foreign Mission Board, Southern Baptist
Convention.   He expressed the opinion that if the
American church "were in Orleans, or at least not too
far from some French homes, missionary work might be
started among the French people, and later on, if and
when American troops leave France, they might leave
some permanent Christian witness in Orleans."[35]
Vincent was quick to realize that his Baptist Federation could profit from the aid of the energetic and
affluent Americans, especially if, as he imagined, the
Americans would one day leave France.   The Southern
Baptist Convention warmed to the idea of becoming
involved in France, and sent Jack Hancox in 1960 to
assume the pastorate of the American congreation in
Orleans, where nearly 10,000 American servicemen were
stationed.   Henceforth the American Baptists in the
military considered the needs of their French co-
religionists when they established English-speaking
churches in Chateauroux, Chambley, Evereux, Laon,
Rueil-Malmaison, Toul, and Verdun.   Each church was
admitted to the French Baptist Federation. One of the
primary benefits brought by the Americans was financial aid.   The American churches designated 45% of
their combined $53,000 budget to the missions program
of the French Baptist Federation, and took regular
offerings for the French work.[36]   American money
lay behind the construction of two large church buildings in Orleans and Chateauroux.

    But French national policy prompted a dramatic
change for the Southern Baptist work in France. President de Gaulle's pursuit of an independent foreign
policy led to the decision of the French government to
request American military forces to leave France,
bringing to a sudden end the thriving English-language
Baptist churches. As pastor Vincent had hoped, the
Americans had made a lasting contribution to French
Baptists both through their years of cooperation and
through the buildings which were left to the French
Baptists. At the final service of the American church
at La Fere near the air base at Laon, the French
pastor remarked that the local French newspaper cited
the cooperation between the American and French
Baptists as an exception to the usual aloofness
between the American military and the French citizens.
When the larger Orleans church was transferred to the
French on January 29, 1967, the event received

national radio and television coverage as an example of Franco-American friendship.[37]

In conclusion of this chapter on the second decade of American evangelical missionary work in France, four developments warrant discussion. First, the number of American missionaries in France continued to grow rapidly, but so did the attrition rate as a number of missionaries abandoned their plans to serve in France. To some extent the increase in attrition went along with the increase in the number of missionaries. As more mission boards came to the conclusion that France was a valid mission field, and as more men and women took an interest in going to France, it became apparent that some of the new recruits lacked the zeal and dedication of the pioneer missionaries. On the other hand, some of the pioneers, evaluating their work over a long period of time felt discouraged, and decided that they could serve better elsewhere. France developed a reputation as a missionary graveyard.

Missionary attrition had been a subject of intensive study by individual mission boards and by inter-mission agencies. But in spite of the compilation of a large body of statistics, it is difficult to arrive at valid conclusions.[38] A study made in the 1950's surveyed the opinions of 915 missionaries from sixteen mainline Protestant denominations who had left service in mission fields around the world. The two most commonly given reasons for a decision to leave were: 1) the ill health of the missionary or a member of his family (24.9%) and 2) disturbed political conditions in the field (24.8%).[39] These figures merely indicated that most of the missionaries surveyed worked in third world nations with a tropical climate and volatile politics. Neither reason did much to explain the attrition in France. Studies made by evangelical mission boards with personnel in France were not much clearer.[40] Most of these reports produced little more than columns of figures gathered from different mission fields. A few samples: Baptist Mid-Missions reported the loss of sixteen missionaries in France between 1947 and 1974, while in the same time losing nine in Ghana, ten in Japan, and twenty in the Central African Republic.[41] The Conservative Baptists, between 1964 and 1974 saw 36% of their

missionaries in France leave, while 25% left
Japan.[42] In twenty years, the Greater European
Mission suffered nearly sixty resignations. Some of
these, however, occurred before overseas service
began. Other studies, presumably using a different
definition of "drop-outs" came up with a lower over-
all rate of 6.8% of groups of over one thousand missionaries world-wide, representing over thirty agencies.[43] France was usually one of the countries
from which attrition was highest, but comparison shed
little light. Although, for instance, attrition
figures for France might be similar to those from,
say, northern Brazil, the reasons could be quite different. One was an unreceptive society with comfortable living conditions, while the other might be far
more receptive, but very uncomfortable. And while
reasons might be listed, it is difficult to sort out
reasons and excuses. Internal mission strife and personality problems were often masked. The decision to
leave, however, was limited to the question of missionary service in France, and rarely, if ever,
included leaving the fold of evangelical Christianity.
Those who returned to America usually assumed positions in evangelical churches or organizations. A few
chose a kind of cultural and geographic compromise,
and worked as missionaries in Quebec. The missionaries never seemed to doubt their basic beliefs and
commitment, but only their place of service.

Reliable information on the number of departures
from France and on the exact reasons for departure is
virtually impossible to obtain. Sometimes the decision to leave was made for family reasons such as the
education of children. Sometimes there was a call of
a more productive ministry in the United States to
which the missionaries returned. But more important
than the actual figure was the widespread notion that
France was a mission field which claimed many casual-
ties. And whatever the primary reason given for a
missionary departure, underlying many decisions to
leave France was the frustration caused by the dis-
couragingly slow progress.

Highly motivated and optimistic in their decision
to go to France, the missionaries often found it difficult to cope with the failure to fulfill their
aspirations. Amid reports of the encouraging success
of missionary work around the world stood the stark
reality of the often stagnant work in France. Continually rebuffed in door-to-door distribution, laboring

in tent campaigns to which few French people came, struggling with groups which failed to grow or even coalesce, the missionaries felt either pesonal spiritual inadequacy or cultural unadaptability or both. Their rejection by French society often made them decide to remain in the apartment and read the Bible or a book about French culture. However, these periods of withdrawal and study would lead to feelings of guilt that the work was not being done, so the missionary would go back to the streets with renewed determination. Rejection and frustration would occur again, and the vicious circle continued. Some decided to go home. And those who stayed were confronted continually by the challenge and temptation that others had left.

However, the second decade of American missionary work in France was marked by achievement as well as attrition. Most significant was the cooperation of American missionaries and French evangelicals in the creation of an evangelical theological seminary in 1965 at Vaux-sur-Seine, twenty miles west of Paris. This was a significant step. Not only was it evidence of the cordiality between the American and French evangelicals which would have been impossible ten or twenty years before, but it also marked a major change in the strategy of each. Originally, the Americans had felt that the evangelization of France would be accomplished rapidly by whirlwind efforts and mass evangelistic rallies which would produce enthusiastic response to the "sowing of the seed". The French evangelicals, on the other hand, had assumed that their modest methods and old institutions were satisfactory for doing the job. Two decades of American missionary work caused both to reassess their positions. The American vision, energy, and stress upon numbers made the French evangelicals aware of the inadequacy of their own progress. The Americans, abandoning the strategy of emergency evangelism, settled in for the long struggle of producing viable French evangelical churches. Both sides realized that a strong evangelical community in France would need to reproduce some pastors and educators who possessed a higher level of academic training than that offered in the Bible School curriculum at Nogent or Lamorlaye, as valuable as those institutions were thought to be in the training of Christian workers. The evangelicals decided to establish a new seminary because they concluded that the two Protestant seminaries in Paris and Montpellier which served the French Reformed church

96

were dominated by liberal theology, and because the little sectarian seminary at Aix-en-Provence had failed because of dependence upon American funds, its combative posture, and an erosion of a broad-based evangelical position.

The seminary at Vaux occupied a large tree-shaded estate in a tranquil setting on the north bank of the Seine. Committed by statutes and pledges to a thoroughly evangelical theology, the Faculté Libre de Théologie Evangélique opened in the fall of 1965 with John Winston, Jr. as dean. Raised in Europe as the son of the American missionary who directed the Belgian Gospel Mission's Bible Institute in Brussels, Winston enjoyed the respect of the American and French evangelical groups. Under his tutelage the school grew in numbers and in prestige. While the seminary maintained a positive, academic, and irenic posture, its enrollment grew from five the first term to over fifty by 1975. After a decade the school had seen nearly all of its one hundred graduates assume positions in full-time evangelical work. Job offers from the French, Swiss, and Belgian Protestant communities far exceeded the numbers of candidates.[44]

Evangelical education in Francophone Europe relied upon five schools: the seminary at Vaux, and Bible institutes at Lamorlaye, Nogent, Brussels, and Vevey, Switzerland (Emmaus Bible Institute). Four of the five schools were directed by an American.

Third, the second decade of missionary work saw the publication of an important book. Convinced about the need to place before American Christians the spiritual condition of Europe, Robert Evans, founder of the European Bible Institute and the Greater Europe Mission, wrote Let Europe Hear, published in 1963.[45] Clearly and forcefully written in a fluid and engaging style, the carefully researched volume offered a country-by-country discussion of the secular and religious factors which had contributed to what evangelicals viewed as the spiritual malaise of Europe. Over five hundred pages in length, Let Europe Hear was at once a historial essay, a contemporary analysis, and an energetic appeal for additional missionaries to France and other European countries.

While Evans was praised for his comprehensive research in literary and historical sources, not all agreed with his conclusions.[46] The most severe criticism pointed out that Evans' book, like most of the American missionaries, ignored or dismissed the evangelicals within the established Protestant and Catholic churches in Europe. A number of French evangelicals claimed the book was outdated, especially where statistics and observations painted such a bleak picture of French Christianity. Indeed, Evans countered by expressing the hope that his figures were being made obsolete by a rapid expansion of evangelical Christianity. Notwithstanding some quibbling about statistics, the message of the book was clear: in spite of its sophisticated civilization and veneer of religion, Europe should be considered more pagan than Asia or Africa, and hence was in dire need of qualified missionaries.

In the succeeding years Evans' book was probably the most important single factor in the formation of the attitudes which prospective missionaires held about France. The 1960's would see the greatest influx of missionaries yet, and almost all read <u>Let Europe Hear</u> before going to France. A significant number made their decision to become missionaries to France because of what they learned from the book. For others who had already decided to go, <u>Let Europe Hear</u> was the cornerstone of their cultural and histor- ical preparation. Most of the American missionaries who came to France since the publication of the book arrived with Evans' thoughts in their minds.

Finally, the second decade of American missionary work in France saw most missions engaged in a deliberate search for a strategy for their evangelical mission. The first decade and a good portion of the second decade had witnessed much aimless activity. This was partly because some American missions had paid no heed to strategy in any of their work around the world. But other organizatins had come to France with an evangelistic strategy which was well-proven elsewhere, only to see it fail miserably in France. Street preaching and teen-age projects were prime examples.

The search for strategy gradually led most missions to the conclusions that they could have a viable and enduring effect upon France only if they established indigenous French churches capable eventually of standing on their own with no missionary assistance. Some missions, like TEAM, made a decisive and clearly delineated commitment to church planting in the late 1950's. Others, like the Greater Europe Misson, more or less slid into the conviction that evangelism should lead to churches. By the late 1960's there were very few American missions in France which did not subscribe to a basic strategy of establishing churches. Even service missions involved in activities like literature distribution, while not engaged actively in church planting, would nonetheless take care to portray their work as related to that basic goal. The churches envisioned were to be mission-sponsored and mission-controlled, usually independent of denominational affiliation. This narrowly sectarian approach denied the American missionaries a larger identity with the symbols and institutions of Christiandom in France. In a secularized and even de-Christianized society this made communication and achievement of their church planting objectives more difficult.

But, there was a big difference between announcing a strategy of church planting and actually working toward establishing a new church. Not all avowed church planters were planting churches. Almost none of them possessed any experience in this activity before going to France, where it was certain to be more difficult. So, the broad-based agreement upon strategy led to an intensive debate about tactics. If the second decade of American missionary work in France was a search for strategy, the third decade would be a search for tactics.

CHAPTER IV NOTES

[1]"Billy's Conquest," _Newsweek_, July 12, 1954, p. 68.

[2]Young, p. 7.

[3]John Jesberg, newsletter, June 15, 1955, TEAM; James Burroughs, "Report on France," Conservative Baptist Foreign Missions Society, 1962.

[4]_Decision_, August 1963, Billy Graham Evangelistic Association, p. 11; _Christianity Today_, July 20, 1963, p. 31.

[5]"Guide Plan for France," 1963, TEAM, p. 1.

[6]_Ibid_.

[7]Schram, p. 128.

[8]Letter, Arthur Johnston to David Johnson, May 17, 1960, TEAM.

[9]Kane, p. 540.

[10]Budd, p. 104.

[11]James Burroughs, "Report on France," CBFMS, 1962; letter, Arthur Johnston to David Johnson, May 17, 1960, TEAM.

[12]Letter from John Jesberg to Vernon Mortenson, January 3, 1957; _Missionary Broadcaster_, March 1957, TEAM, p. 10.

[13]Frances Johnston, unpublished manuscript, TEAM publication office files.

[14]Randall Mathews, newsletter, December 1965, CBFMS.

[15]Allen, p. 25.

[16]See McGavran, _Understanding Church Growth_ (Grand Rapids: Eerdmans, 1970); Marty, _The Public Church_ (New York: Crossroad, 1981), pp. 77-79.

[17]Interview with Richard Winchell, associate general director of TEAM, February 2, 1973.

[18]1962 Annual Conference Report, TEAM; Ivan Peterson, newsletters, May, 1969, July, 1963, TEAM.

[19]Sheetz, p. 198.

[20]Sheetz, p. 196.

[21]"Report of the Church Organization Committee," Annual Report 1956, p. 14, Greater Europe Mission (GEM).

[22]Roger Mehl, Traite de sociologie du protestantisme (Neuchatel: Delachaux and Niestle, 1965), pp. 209, 210; Seguy, Les sects protestantes dans la France contemporaine (Paris: Beauchesne, 1956), pp. 80-81, 92-95, 117, 141, 162, 170, 174, 178, 284.

[23]David Moberg, The Church as a Social Institution (Englewood Cliffs, N.J.: Prentice Hall, 1962), p. 74; on church-sect typology see Ernst Troeltsch, The Social Teaching of the Christian Churches, trans. Olive Wyon (London: George Allen and Unwin, 1931), I, pp. 331-381, II, pp. 993-1013, cited Ibid.

[24]The Missionary Herald, 1957, National Fellowship of Brethren Churches, p. 485.

[25]See Edward McCreary's view of American businessmen in Europe, The Americanization of Europe (Garden City: Doubleday, 1964).

[26]Randall Mathews, newsletter, July, 1964, CBFMS; 1966 Annual Conference Report, TEAM, p. 36.

[27]1968 Annual Conference Report, TEAM, p. 3; "Report of the Christian Junior-Senior High School Project Committee," GEM, 1967.

[28]Maisie Ward, France Pagan? The Mission of Abbe Godin, (New York: Sheed and Ward, 1949).

[29]J. Petrie (Robert J. Petrie Hewison), The Worker Priests, A Collective Documentation, (London: Routledge and Kegan Paul, 1956).

101

[30]"Chateau de Saint-Albain," 1967, NFBC, p. 1.

[31]1962 Annual Report, p. 220; 1967 Annual Report, p. 31, MBMC.

[32]"History of the Alpine Mission to France," paper in files of the Unevangelized Fields Mission, Bala-Cynwyd, Pennsylvania.

[33]Jane Bernardo, newsletter, 1954, UFM.

[34]E. Barde, L'Evangélisation Rurale en France, 1947, pp. 93-102, cited in World Council of churches, "Evangelism in France", p. 45.

[35]Lewis M. Krause, Scattered Abroad: The Story of English Language Baptist Work in Europe (Heidelberg: Herstellung-Brausdruck, 1966), p. 27.

[36]Krause, pp. 41, 42.

[37]European Baptist Press Service, Ruschlikon, Switzerland, October 3, 1966, no. 66:207; February 8, 1967, no. 67:45.

[38]"Why They Come Home", Evangelical Missions Quarterly, Winter, 1967, pp. 119-121; Kane, Winds of Change, p. 56.

[39]Moyer, p. 54; See also Helen Bailey and Herbert Jackson, A Study of Missionary Motivation, Training, and Withdrawal (1953-1962) (New York: Missionary Research Library, 1965).

[40]Letter from Raymond Buck, Baptist Mid-Missions, to the author, March 20, 1974; letter from Arno Enns, Conservative Baptist Foreign Mission Society to the author, March 20, 1974; letter from Al Larson, Unevangelized Fields Mission to the author, May 23, 1974.

[41]Letter from Buck, March 20, 1974.

[42]Letter from Larson, May 23, 1974.

[43]"Why They Come Home", Evangelical Missions Quarterly, Winter, 1967, p. 119.

[44]"Europe's New Evangelical Seminaries," _Christianity Today_, April 28, 1972, Vol. XVI, no. 15, p. 39; letter from John Winston to the author, August 10, 1976.

[45]Robert Evans, _Let Europe Hear_ (Chicago: Moody Press, 1963).

[46]Martin Marty, _Varieties of Unbelief_, p. 101

CHURCH PLANTING, MORE OR LESS, 1965-1975

The story of American evangelical missionary work in France between 1965 and 1975 saw not only a continuing increase in the number of missionaries, but also a steady rise in the number of mission boards which for the first time decided to send their missionaries to France. The strategy discussions of the late 1950's and the early 1960's had led most missions to the conclusion that they could best influence French society by establishing indigenous evangelical churches. As this strategy became more clearly defined, most missions tried to ensure that their various activities in France were somehow related to the primary task of planting and nurturing churches.

The increased concern with church planting and church growth was in accord with the ideas of missionary theoretician Donald McGavran, of Fuller Theological Seminary in South Pasadena, California. His philosophy and programs for church growth became widely accepted in many mission endeavors throughout the evangelical world. Stressing that the growth of Christianity was linked directly to the growth of indigenous local churches, McGavran insisted that much missionary work was unproductive and ill-conceived. Through his many publications, but especially his influential Understanding Church Growth (Grand Rapids: William B. Eerdmans Publishing Co., 1970), McGavran attacked the fuzzy thinking so prevalent in missionary circles. The central task of missions, he wrote, was "the effective multiplication of churches in the receptive societies of the earth."[1] Instead of this, he said, too many missionaries busied themselves in "general mission work," "outreach," "evangelism," or "witness." These terms were devoid of content, and usually masked unproductive activity. Unless missionaries devoted themselves to organizing their converts into a congregation which grew, McGavran warned, their effort would be wasted. As he challenged missions to focus upon the establishment of new churches, McGavran urged the use of the hitherto neglected tools of sociology and anthropology to facilitate missionary work. As many missionaries in France embraced the ideas of the church growth movement, they became both inspired and frustrated. Inspiration and confidence came with the realization that at last they had a clear strategy. But frustration came once again when they compared church planting and church growth in France with other mission fields. Reports from places like Bolivia where forty-one new churches with 450 newly baptized members were started in three months made the progress in France look miniscule.[2] McGavran's ideas took root best in non-Christian areas of the third world, not in post-Christian Europe. The church growth movement in missions did not come to grips with the problems faced by immature missionary work in a society with ancient Christian churches and traditions. Furthermore, and perhaps more distressing, McGavran's ideas called for missions to concentrate their efforts toward church growth only in those societies which were receptive. Priorities had to be set. There was too much to do, he said, and too many peoples receptive to evangelism for mission boards to assign personnel and money to unproductive areas. No one could claim that France was a receptive society for missionaries. So, while the church growth movement gave the missionaries in France a plan for action, it also undermined their entire effort.

One of the prominent features of American missionary work in France in these years was the multiplication of Baptist mission agencies working in France. Within a decade five new Baptist missions sent personnel to France. Most of them had identical aspirations and beliefs, but they did little in cooperation with one another. The largest group of new missionaries came under the banner of the Conservative Baptist Foreign Mission Society. Their first missionaries to France arrived on the rebound from the Congo. Surprisingly, Congolese politics was to be a factor in determining the evangelical missionary population of France. The political and military crisis in 1960-62 which accompanied the independence of the Congo made it impossible for most American missionaries to continue their work in the new African state. The missionaries were forced to find other places to work. Since they had been trained in the French language, often in Paris, a number decided to shift their field of missionary service from Africa to France. They were not dissuaded by the great cultural difference between Africa and France. These people were, above all else, missionaries. Viewing the world through theological lenses, evangelical missionaries tended to see little distinction between mission fields, except for the willingness of peoples to embrace Christianity. By this standard France was a more difficult field of service than Africa. The French, who held their national culture in highest esteem, were slow to understand the missionary point of view on this issue.

The first Conservative Baptist missionaries to France, James and Beverly Burroughs, had just completed one term in the Belgian Congo when they moved into a working class neighborhood in the northern Paris suburb of Arnouville-les-Gonesse. Their sectarian view of their "pioneer" mission came across clearly in their first newsletter from France in which they claimed to be not only the first American family to live in that town, but also "perhaps the first Christians in modern times."[3]

As additional Counservative Baptist missionaries arrived in France, emerged from language study, and began their work, they demonstrated considerable confusion about methods, policies, and goals. They expended a great deal of effort writing elaborate plans which proposed one kind of evangelistic activity or another. The missionaries displayed a persistent inability to decide upon the nature of the Conservative Baptist Foreign Mission Society's relationship with the French Baptist groups: should they remain independent, should they affiliate, could they cooperate with each other? Having run into problems in attempting to pursue each of these courses, they made no specific decision except for a vague general policy of "collaboration" with French Baptists.[4]

There was also persistent and discouraging failure to see positive results from evangelistic efforts. The missionaries were working against themselves. Low response to their message served to convince the merely disinterested that their cause was unworthy, and that evangelical Christianity could not succeed in French culture. Their persistent attempts in an area of marginal interest led only to a general rejection. Although the missionaries took solace in their perseverance, the more they worked, the less they could achieve. Having obviously failed to attract even a small following, the missionaries' continued efforts promoted negative impressions, contributing to a neighborhood consensus against the work.

By 1970, their numbers having risen to twenty, missionaries from the Conservative Baptist Foreign Mission Society had been in France for eight years, but had little to show for their efforts. Only one tiny church group, moved from a one-car garage in

Arnouville-les-Gonesse to a two-car garage in Villiers-le-Bel, showed any signs of growth and maturity. But the reliance of this assembly upon women and foreigners concerned those hopeful of establishing a strong church.[5] It was difficult to engender a sense of prestige when baptisms took place in a plastic child's pool placed outside the garage window.[6]

Although all American evangelical missionaries to France experienced a considerable lack of success, the record of the Conservative Baptist Foreign Mission Society in the 1960's was unusually meager. The neighborhoods in which they chose to work appeared to be as resistant as any encountered in France. The missionaries rarely found people who were interested in attending Bible studies or services. And even when they were successful in bringing a small group together for study and discussion, it would fall apart in a short time. The French, they concluded, even when interested in Christianity, were reluctant to attend regular meetings for more than a few weeks or months. Religion in modern France, even if taken seriously, was not a full-time commitment.[7] Whether because of the habit of perfunctory Catholic ritual, or the heritage of the hidden Huguenots, or the secularization of society, the devout in France tended to hide their lamp under a bushel.

Above all, the Conservative Baptist Foreign Mission Society failed to agree upon a specific strategy. Behind the general slogan of church planting there was little plan of exactly how that was to be accmplished. The missionaries became increasingly discouraged. As they kept track of their seminary classmates who were pastoring large churches in America, some wondered if they were wasting their time. Continually concerned about strategy, yet unable to agree upon a unified approach, the Conservative Baptist missionaries entered the 1970's doggedly continuing their work in unresponsive locations. With Hugh Collins doing evangelism and David Dixon assuming pastoral duties, the church in Villiers-le-Bel grew steadily, if slowly. By 1975 the number of baptized believers had reached thirty, and the attendance figure approached sixty. Conversions came slowly. However, not all those who professed conversion became church members. In fact, many of the new members of the Villiers-le-Bel church were transfers from other evangelical groups. And a large number were foreigners or were French citizens from the West Indies islands of Martinique and Guadaloupe.

Here were three common problems for the American missionaries in France. First, conversions, rare as they were, often failed to lead to church membership. Second, much of the church growth which did occur was transfer growth. Usually the transfers were part of the large number of French citizens who left the provinces and flocked to the huge Parisian urban sprawl.[8] Sometimes, however, people transferred from local churches, and this could cause hard feelings between the pastors. Finally, the American missionaries to France found that their new churches were often based upon foreigners. Settling in France in increasing numbers in the 1960's, immigrants from Europe, Africa, and French overseas territories proved more receptive than native Frenchmen to religious overtures from Catholics and Protestants alike.[9] It was not unusual, especially in the Paris region, for missionary-established churches to include a significant number of black Antillians.

Another aspect of the mission's effort in France was a research project employing a sociological survey of conversion experiences of French believers. The American missionaries had not yet bothered to consult the respected French scholarship in religious sociology. Some of their problems might have been avoided, or at least explained, if they had been aware of the correlations drawn by Le Bras and then Boulard between religious practice, geography, occupation, and social milieu.[10] A few missionaries disclaimed missionary strategy based upon sociological research as "unspiritual," but many were interested in the research and hoped that it would be the long-sought key to opening French society to evangelical Christianity. However, some missionaries maintained that the research had yielded some intriguing ideas, but that all the new proposals and ideas had produced little tangible results. The rest of the Conservative Baptist missionaries kept plugging away in the stark new apartment clusters in Marne-la-Vallée, finding some receptivity, mainly among Antillians and Portugese in the communities of Torcy and Ozoir-la-Ferrière.[11]

Next on the list of Baptist mission agencies entering France in the 1960's was the National Association of Free Will Baptists. Enjoying generous

American financial support, the Free Will Baptist missionaries started small churches in Nantes and Rennes.

The other Baptist mission boards operating in France were usually fundamentalist and separatist in policies and practices. Their brochures stressed what they opposed as much as what they supported. These missions took aim at neo-orthodoxy, neo-evangelicalism, ecumenism, liberalism, and pentecostalism. They were determined to bring to France the secondary and divisive issues of American fundamentalism. In spite of the miniscule evangelical population of France, some of these fundamentalist missions seemed to be very much concerned with teaching their tiny groups of French evangelicals about the need for separation from Christian groups of different convictions. The Evangelical Baptist Missions sent personnel to Marseilles, Toulon, Fountainbleu, and Melun.[12] Baptist International Missions, Incorporated (Chattanooga) supported missionaries in Argenteuil and Sens. Baptist World Missions sponsored a meager effort near Metz.

Another small separatist mission, the Worldwide European fellowship (born out of the disintegrating European Evangelistic Crusade) saw less success and even more trouble than most missions in France. Their missionaries had acquired a large tent in which to conduct their itinerant evangelism throughout the country. They spent much of their time wrestlng with the tent, guarding it, and moving it from place to place. In the Paris region they had difficulty finding appropriate sites for the tent. In traditionally Catholic Brittany there was almost no response, and sometimes no attendance. In the south the Mediterranean winds frequently threatened to blow down the tent. Ultimately a decision was reached to concentrate the work in Alsace where it was less breezy, and where the German Protestant heritage produced a more receptive atmosphere.[13] Although the crowds were larger in cities like Colmar, Mulhouse, and Strasbourg, the response was proportionately small, in spite of the increased time, energy and funds invested by the American mission. Gradually the mission turned its attention to the goal of establishing an indigenous church in Besancon, a graceful but growing city along the Doubs in Franche-Comte. As usual, progress was very slow, made even slower by dissension within the mission and the attrition of its missionaries.[14]

Several other American missions also began their work in France in the late 1960's. America's most established pentecostal denomination, the Assemblies of God, decided to add France to the list of countries targeted by the denomination's foreign mission office in Springfield, Missouri. Attempting to combine evangelism with providing aid to teenagers, the Assemblies of God opened Teen Challenge France in a coffee bar next to the Seine in the Latin Quarter, and won national press and television commendation for its effort to assist teens caught up in the growing Parisian drug problem. The most distinctive aspect of the Assemblies of God missionaries involved French gypsies. In the mid-1960's the French Assemblies of God churches sparked a revival within the gypsy community which attracted over five thousand gypsies to join the Assemblies of God.[15]

Although the Assemblies of God missionaries in France experienced a measure of success, they found themselves in a strange and at times an isolated position. Even though they and the other American missionaries held similar convictions about the basic evangelical gospel, the pentecostal emphasis of the Assemblies of God made many evangelicals wary of them. Theological concerns were coupled with the possibility that the already small evangelical groups might lose members to proselytizing pentecostals. Doctrinal differences, suspicion, and even hostility kept distance between the Assemblies of God missionaries and the other Americans. On the other hand, the American Assemblies of God missionaries did not find a warm reception from the local French Assemblies of God pastors. Even though the French Assemblies of God traced their origin to British and American missionary intervention in 1930, they seemed little inclined to develop a partnership with the American missionaries of the post-war period.[16] By all accounts the French pentecostals were the fastest-growing Christian group in France, and the singular strength of the French Assemblies of God movement caused some of them to question the need for these American missionaries.

Strangely enough, one of the largest groups of American missionaries in France (34 by 1975) developed little contact with the French people. The North Africa Mission, with its headquarters in Upper Darby, Pennsylvania, had labored in Muslim North Africa since 1881. In 1963, as the political climate of North

Africa made work there increasingly difficult, the North Africa Mission moved its African office and many of its missionaries to nearby southern France. From here they beamed radio broadcasts across the Mediterranean to North Africa. Although there were over one million North African Muslims in France, surpassing, perhaps, the Protestant population, not until 1970 did the mission begin a small evangelization effort with the North African population in the French cities of Mareille, St. Etienne, and Grenoble.[17]

Campus Crusade for Christ was one of the fastest growing evangelical organizations in the world in the late 1960's. From its headquarters near San Bernadino, California, Campus Crusade supervised a far-flung and energetic student evangelism effort. Its simple evangelistic strategy was based upon "the four spiritual laws," a little gospel tract which was to be read to potential converts. Although the mission's accomplisments among French university students were minimal, the mission distinguished itself in a small way by when its first missionary enrolled in language training at Chambon-sur-Lignon. This Protestant community was among the most widely known religious centers in France. Worldwide acclaim had come to the village and its pastor Andre Trocmé for their heroic protection of Jews during the German occupation of World War II.[18] The postwar Cévenol school and conferences attracted a steady stream of world Protestant leaders to the tiny village high in the rugged Massif Central. But the American missionaries shunned the place.

Finally, among the missions new to France in the 1960's there was one which departed from the practice of starting new churches. The Gospel Missionary Union established a policy which insisted that the American missionaries serve as assistants to French evangelical pastors, rather than initiating new and independent American-sponsored ministries. By the mid-1970's the Missouri-based mission sponsored sixteen missionaries who had affiliated with five existing congregations of the small Eglise Libre denomination.[19] The Gospel Missionary Union did not boast a large mission in France, and its working philosophy earned the acclaim of the French evangelicals. By assuming positions under the authority of a local French pastor, Gospel Missionary Union missionaries usually avoided offending French cultural sensitivity, and they also avoided much of the anti-American feeling which at times hindered other missions. Whether this policy was the most efficient use of American personnel in France remained a subject for debate in missionary circles. Some American critics said that the decision to subordinate the missionaries to French pastoral leadership stifled or wasted American energy, time, and Yankee know-how. Other observers, more attuned to long-range goals and qualitative rather than quantitative assessment, applauded the Gospel Missionary Union's approach. The identification of the mission with a specific French denomination eased many of the problems of cultural acceptance, but the choice of so small a denomination limited severely the impact of a wise strategic decision.

While it is true that a distinguishing feature of American missionary work in France in the late 1960's and early 1970's was the marked increase in the number of mission agencies just beginning to operate in France, the period also brought noteworthy developments in the work of the older missions.

The mid-1960's brought change to the Grace Brethren mission in France. Having obtained a new strategy and an old chateau in 1964, the Grace Brethren missionaries spent the next decade attempting to implement the "chateau experiment," under the leadership of Thomas Julien. The basic idea was "to see whether, in a de-Christianized area having no evangelical tradition, it is faster to evangelize and establish churches by working through a neutral center than by the traditional method of each missionary independently beginning a work and trying to develop it into a church. The chateau is essentially a bridge between the people and the church."[20]

The "chateau experiment" was an attempt to deal with the two basic questions for the missionary venture in France: (1) What was the place of the Christian church in French society? (2) What was the relationship of the American missionaries to the church in France? Most American missionaries did not appreciate the ambivalence with which the French viewed their church. French society included some extremists who either unquestioningly followed the church or unsympathetically rejected it. But most Frenchmen, while sometimes revering the church and sometimes reviling the church, usually merely ignored the church. France had become a secular society, but had secularization processed to the point of complete de-Christianization? If French society had become de-Christianized, the church's position in France would be anachronistic, its role dysfunctional, and its image negative. American missionary efforts would be crippled by their association with an institution which had been rejected by most of French society. Juilien's chateau strategy reflected his conclusion that de-Christianization in France was so pervasive that religion could attract Frenchmen only if it disassociated itself from institutional churches. The religious Americans and the secular French would meet on the neutral ground of the chateau.

However, judgment of a nation's religious beliefs is unsure, and the verdict subject to appeal. While Julien perceived the large gulf between the church and much of de-Christianized French society, and came up with a plan for bridging it, others pointed out that the Christian church had proven its resilience in France over the centuries. In spite of progressive and pervasive secularization, most Frenchmen refused to renounce the church entirely. Ignoring the church for most of their days, they nonetheless returned for the milestones of life: baptism, marriage, and burial. And in this secular society the notion lingered that if there was going to be any religion, it should come from the church. To reach the people who felt this way about the church, missionaries needed a closer relationship and identity with the French church. Of course, for most Frenchmen the church was the Roman Catholic church, and the Protestant American evangelical missionaries were hamstrung by their almost complete refusal to have anything to do with the Catholic church. However, the Reformed church in France still enjoyed a measure of respect and influence. For those who determined that secular France was still part of Christendom, the Reformed church afforded the opportunity for evangelical Protestants to be identified with traditional and established Christianity in France.

But most of the American missionaries tended to ignore these two basic views of the Christian church in France. Accepting neither the strength of de-Christianization nor the strength of church tradition in France, most missions pursued policies which cut them off from adherents of either view. Their small, sectarian, separatist groups were too much like the church for some Frenchmen, too little like the church for other Frenchmen. Not surprisingly the few whom the missionaries attracted were usually those on the margin of French society.

As with other missionary work in France, work at the chateau went very slowly at first, and the missionaries found themselves spending as much time in physical repair of the building as in spiritual repair of French souls. Their initial plan was to establish the identity of the chateau as an evangelical center, and within a year the chateau proved to be a popular retreat site. The chateau-based strategy seemed to be an answer to some of the problems of evangelical work in France, especially those which stemmed from the missionaries' lack of identity and status. It allowed local Christians to identify with something larger than a store-front gospel hall or a chapel in a garage. But it also avoided the stamp of the formal, institutional Christianity which had become distasteful to so many Frenchmen. The chateau's ample facilities and its central location along the Paris-Lyon-Marseille auto route led to its increasing use as a Christian conference center. But the chateau ministry was intended to lead directly to the establishment of local churches, and this was not being achieved readily. The small evangelical groups in nearby Chalon and Macon remained weak. Julien became concerned that the successful chateau programs might eclipse the primary goal of starting churches, and he continually stressed the importance of the chateau as a means to achieve that goal, and not an end in itself.[21] Although progress in church planting had been slow, the respected missionary leader was convinced that his strategy was correct for a de-Christianized society. By 1975 the value of the chateau as a conference center was well attested, but there was not yet a clear verdict on its role as a bridge to new churches.

One of the oldest missions in France made a big change in its tactics. The Alpine Mission (now merged with the Unevangelized Fields Mission) came to realize that its choice of location was important, and that it had chosen the wrong place. Rural evangelism in the valleys of the French Alps, missionaries trudging from village to village with packets of Scriptures, had yielded little success. Diligent plodding had become the spirit of the Alpine Mission to France. Changes came when leadership of the mission passed to

James Nesbitt, who had become interested in missionary work in France when he studied in Paris on a Fulbright scholarship.[22] Alpine evangelism gave way to an urban focus. Nesbitt moved to Valence, and within a year he had been instrumental in organizing a church of forty members, with between seventy and eighty in regular attendance. The rapid growth was chiefly due to the presence of a number of evangelicals in the city who were anxious for leadership; the church coalesced, rather than grew. Nesbitt pastored the congregation for more than three years until the church, by then formally affiliated with the Eglise Libre, called a French pastor. Growth continued, and by 1975 over 120 were attending Sunday services.[23]

Next, the mission opened a student center near the university in Grenoble. The project was distinctive in two ways. First, the missionaries, as many as nine at one time, worked as a team, with their activities closely coordinated. The idea of individual missionaries pecking away at their own little projects was determined a waste of time and personnel. Second, the work of the American missionaries was coordinated with and even made subordinant to a local French church, a dynamic Brethren assembly known as the Foyer Evangélique. Its pastor, Marcel Tabailloux, had won a reputation as one of the most energetic and knowledgeable young evangelical leaders in France. Partnership with his church not only gave the missionary work the appearance of being French-directed, but also afforded them the invaluable counsel and leadership of Tabailloux. It was a mutually beneficial arrangement which disproved a widespread notion that French pastors and American missionaries made poor partners. At least in this case their energies and talents were complementary and productive.

The Unevangelized Fields Mission effort in Grenoble rapidly became one of the most promising missionary projects in France. It owed as much of its success to its highly motivated and capable personnel as it did to the wisdom of strategic and organizational decisions. The mainstays of the work, Sutherland Maclean, Ronald Fisher, and Henry Bryant, had been well prepared for working with university students. Most American missionaries had been educated in conservative Christian colleges or Bible schools, with an intellectual and social atmosphere different from that of a secular university. They usually felt uneasy with students. However, the Unevangelized Fields Mission men in Grenoble were Princeton graduates (as was field leader Nesbitt) who were familiar with the secular student idiom. They had been exposed to intellectually challenging evangelical groups on their own secular campus. Delighted to find welcome response to their efforts, they often counted one conversion per week. It was clear that after years of plodding work in mountain valleys, the missionaries of the Alpine Mission to France had found more successful and rewarding work. Like many other missionaries in France they discovered that establishing friendships was a prerequisite to successful personal evangelism. Traditional American evangelistic methods like street preaching and literature distribution were impersonal, and had been discredited in France. The student ministry and the local church grew together, and by 1975 Sunday attendance at the Foyer Evangélique had surpassed 100.[24]

The Alpine Mission/Unevangelized Fields Mission work in France was a story of contrast. A small low-key mission plodding along in unproductive rural evangelism had rapidly become involved with dynamic urban churches in Valence and Grenoble. The joint efforts of the American and French had produced some of the most encouraging evangelical growth in France. The work in Grenoble especially deserved the attention, acclaim, and even imitation of other American missionaries and French evangelicals. It was not that the mission had discovered a magic touch. They also worked in Bourg-en-Bresse and Ambérieu where progress still came very slowly. But in Grenoble the conditions were unusually favorable. Perhaps the Franco- American cooperation was as much due to compatible personalities as compatible policies. The missionaries found that students and other young people between the ages of fifteen and twenty-five were more responsive to foreigners and more likely to consider new ideas than any other group in French society. Furthermore, the social climate of Grenoble was more open than that of many other French cities. The sleek modernizing city in the Alps took pride in its new cosmopolitan image, and was accommodating to foreigners.[25]

Of course, the promising evangelical movement in Grenoble was not without weaknesses. Ministries which were heavily dependent upon students had inherent problems. Student discussion groups attracted people

who wanted to talk and never listen. Campus climates
changed quickly, and student groups were volatile.
One year's large and active group could evaporate by
the next year. Diligent effort was required continually to fuse student ministries with the local
church. Furthermore, groups in Grenoble included the
usual high proportion of foreigners, and the active
Grenoble evangelical community saw proven leaders and
potential leaders move away. But notwithstanding the
real and potential problems, there remained the
growing evangelical community of over 150 persons
which the American missionaries and French
evangelicals had brought together.

In the early 1970's new growth came to the two
most prominent American missions in France, the Evangelical Alliance Mission (TEAM) and the European Bible
Institute (Greater Europe Mission). By 1975 TEAM
would point to seven organized churches (three of them
were legally established associations cultuelle) and
five embryonic congregations yielding a combined
weekly church attendance of over six hundred persons.
The number of TEAM missionaries doubled, increasing
from sixteen in 1965 to thirty-three in 1975. TEAM
had become recognized as the most energetic (and some
said the most American) mission in France.

By the mid-1960's the mission had become organized enough to plan in advance its annual program. A
typical year would see summers spent in camp work and
in outdoor meetings for children. Usually the mission
would sponsor a concert given by an American evangelical college glee club on a summer swing through
Europe. Fall began with evangelistic crusades in
Orly, Fresnes, or neighboring towns in the southern
suburbs of Paris, followed by a Bible conference at
Nogent Bible Institute, a conference for Sunday school
teachers, a bateau mouche cruise on the Seine for
young people, a baptismal service, and the missionaries' semi-annual business conference. Winter
brought another round of conferences and rallies, as
well as ski camps and perhaps a concert. Spring was
the time for church picnics on Ascension Day and
Pentecost, planning the summer camps, and the annual
mission conference.[26] The annual conferences
reflected the increasing maturity and order in TEAM's
work in France. Missionaries prepared and delivered
increasingly sophisticated position papers on aspects
of missionary work in French society, and by the mid-
1970's each missionary submitted a lengthy written

personal report and evaluation to which goals for the coming year were appended. But the real work of the missionaries, day by day throughout the year, focused primarily upon the weekly Sunday church services and the mid-week Bible studies: preparing messages and visiting parishioners.

The church in Orly remained at the heart of the TEAM program. The rapid growth of the early 1960's and the enthusiasm over the new building created the optimistic hope, as early as 1965, that a French pastor could be called to lead the church when Arthur Johnston returned to the United States on furlough.[27] This proved an elusive hope. When Johnston went on furlough he was replaced by Robert Vajko who had previously worked at the TEAM church in Fresnes. Several years later, when it was time for Vajko to go on furlough, the pastorate had to be assumed by yet another missionary. This was not encouraging. By 1975 TEAM was still unable to find a French pastor in whose hands they felt they could place the responsibility for a church over which they had labored for almost twenty years.

The retention of American pastors did not mean that the French in the Orly congregation were totally without leadership potential. On the contrary, the deacons in the Orly church established satellite Bible study groups in the neighboring towns of Morangis, Créteil, Longjumeau, Crosnes, and Vigneux. The missionaries planned that the small groups, meeting almost exclusively under French leadership from the Orly church, would eventually become churches in their own right.[28]

In the late 1960's there had been a slackening in the rate of advance, perhaps because of the transition between pastors, or perhaps because the size of the church required the missionary to spend more time in pastoral care and less time in evangelism. This was a common problem in missionary churches. As long-sought church growth began to materialize, more people brought more problems, and the missionary found himself bogged down with intra-church matters. Organizational chores, financial problems, and personality clashes claimed his time. The small group might become a closed circle, preoccupied with their own concerns. Outsiders would find it difficult to penetrate the group. Initial success in church planting could retard or even preclude subsequent growth.

Stagnation occurred, and in some cases disintegration threatened.

But in 1969 the Orly growth rate began to jump dramatically, the impetus coming from an unforeseen quarter. Charles Siounath, a native of the French West Indies island of Guadaloupe, became an evangelical Christian, and shared his conversion experience with his large Antillian family. What followed was a classic example of widespread conversion within the web relationship of a large extended family. Common in many mission fields, such developments were rare in the small tightly-knit family units of France. Within the next three years over fifteen members of the Siounath family were baptised. In the 1970's TEAM found that these Antillians were unquestionably the most responsive group they had discovered in French society. TEAM was not alone in this conclusion. Other missionary churches as well as venerable French evangelical churches saw their numbers swelled by some of the 150,000 Antillian immigrants who lived in the Paris region.[29]

This brought growth pains of an unusual kind. The influx of black Guadaloupians and Martiniquans raised a racial question. Would the average Frenchman be even less inclined to attend an evangelical church in which the more than half the congregation was black? Should the missionaries concentrate their efforts solely on the responsive elements of the society who appreciated their message, ignoring the rest? Or would that tactic give the congregation a foreign stamp and make it less attractive to the bulk of society? Although concerned about these questions, TEAM missionaries directed much of their effort to the responsive Antillian community, where they did not encounter the reserve and resentment with which most native Frenchmen greeted them. With unusual speed the missionaries and Antillians in the Orly church were instrumental in the establishment of three small new churches in Créteil, Brunoy, and Epinay.[30]

TEAM's successful effort with the Antillians led to the most rapid church growth produced by the American missionary effort in France. It was cause for both celebration and concern. Any evangelical growth in France was celebrated as a significant achievement. And the TEAM experience among the Antillian population bolstered the contention of a number of missionaries that the most rapid church growth occurred in homogeneous social groups, particularly minority groups and foreigners. Although Antillians were not foreigners in a technical sense (most held French citizenship), they were a distinct minority group. It had become normal for American missionaries in all regions of France to find greater receptivity among foreigners than among Frenchmen. This prompted second thoughts about the role of missions in France and the role of France in missions. By the mid-1970's most major American mission boards subscribed not only to the church planting strategy, but also to the corollary principle of concentrating their efforts only on receptive peoples. This allowed the missionaries in France to justify their emphasis upon the Antillians, but when the principle was applied to global missionary strategy it could only call into question the allocation of general mission resources to a country as unreceptive as France. The missionaries sought to bring the gospel to any who would respond, but their specific and ultimate goals were to evangelize the French and establish French churches. When they realized that the most successful aspect of their effort was with the non-French peoples, some became concerned about the basic purpose and strategy of their entire mission to France. The missionaries who advocated zealously the strategy of starting new churches among receptive peoples profited from possessing, at least, a definite plan and, more important, the approval of many colleagues in the American evangelical missionary movement around the world. These were the people who shared the missionaries' basic values, and whose support, therefore, was so welcome. But, in France, the propagation of tiny store-front minority group churches made less likely the accomplishment of the missionaries' original avowed objective: an evangelical impact upon the French nation.

The Orly church was the largest of the churches established by missionaries in France. Its congregation numbering over 160 on a Sunday morning was in the minds of many missionaries roughly equivalent to having a church of 1600 in the United States, since a common rule of thumb had been accepted that it took about ten times as much work for one convert in France as for ten in America. But size alone did not make it self-sufficient, and, still paying off an expensive building in 1975, the church saw no immediate prospect of supporting a French pastor. TEAM's primary aim in establishing a church had been convincingly accomplished. Its ultimate aim of withdrawing from a church secure in French hands remained unfulfilled.

The Franco-American umbrella organization created by TEAM to coordinate its ministries in France expanded its own work in the early 1970's and made sporadic progress toward becoming indigenous. The AEEI ordained its first pastor, Marc Descheemaecker in 1966, and saw a gradual increase in the number and role of Frenchmen in the organization. It became the general practice for mission planning sessions first to determine _Alliance_ needs, and then to assign the tasks of TEAM missionaries accordingly. A primary function of the _Alliance_ was the operation of the sea-side conference center acquired at Houlgate on the Normandy coast in 1965.[31] Behind the harmonious cooperation between the French and American members of the AEEI directorate loomed the vital question of the entire TEAM activity in France: when and how was control of the AEEI to be transferred from the American missionaries to the young French pastors? The missionaries had attempted to train their church members for eventual leadership roles, but progress was slow, as Johnston explained in his reports to mission headquarters: "Most French churches seem to lack this basic concept of a healthy utilization of lay members. While we as missionaries don't want to remain too long in the capacity of pastors, yet it becomes more and more apparent that we are going to have to at least lead them out of the initial stages into the program of a growing organization . . .. The evangelization of France, as far as TEAM's responsibility is concerned, is still in the initial stages."[32] It was obvious to the missionaries in the 1970's that it was too soon to turn the missionary project into an independent French church association.

The problem was complicated by a paradox. It was the success of TEAM's church planting and camp ministries which would enable the Americans to transfer their work to the French. But that success, achieved so laboriously, made the mission reluctant to risk its investment of time and funds by relinquishing control to inexperienced French leadership. The history of nineteenth century missions demonstrated that foreign implants in France had trouble surviving, and the missionaries realized that the church should break its American connection as soon as possible. But they also realized that small and weak evangelical groups, French or American, tended to wither.

122

The AEEI was Johnston's attempt to combine American leadership, vision, and control with the structure, counsel, and image of French evangelicalism. In 1975, even after nearly twenty years, it was too soon to assess the ultimate role of the AEEI as a bridge between the mission and indigenous French churches. Although some observers, including leading French evangelicals, gave high acclaim to the magnitude of the TEAM accomplishment and to the growing French role in the AEEI, others, among them American missionaries, claimed that in spite of years of Franco-American work, the image of the group was unquestionably American.[33]

An era in the history of TEAM in France came to an end in 1970 with the decision of field chairman Arthur Johnston to leave France and assume educational positions in America. One of the largest missions in France and perhaps the most influential and visible, TEAM had come a long way from the 1952 baseball games in the Bois de Boulogne. Recognized as the pacesetter in church planting and camp ministry, TEAM owed its achievements to hard work, endurance in spite of far more failure than success, a measure of adaptability to French culture and a measure of resistance to it, and above all to the leadership of Arthur Johnston. The imposing missionary leader in many ways personified TEAM's work in France: aggressive, assertive, and American. From the first day, TEAM's work in France bore the imprint of Johnston's conviction and character. It was he who initially opted for a mission directed at French youth, and it was he who changed the mission's strategy to church planting when he realized that the first five years of youth work had yielded no lasting results. Beginning with the kitchen Bible study in Orly, Johnston provided the leadership which led to the organization of the largest missionary church in France.

If, as some observers claimed, the TEAM churches were too American in flavor, it was because of Johnston's strong feelings about his accountability to the missionaries' American supporters. Their money, he asserted, should be used only to found churches whose creed and format were similar to their own churches at home. Johnston explained this as a form of his accountability to God. Promoting rigid evangelical doctrine was more important to him than cultural adaptation to France. Like most evangelical missionaries

he was convinced that he was involved in the most
important aspect of human history: the extension of
true Christianity. Even though French society as a
whole seemed to have turned against Christianity, this
in no way diminished his responsibility and his task.
Positive, determined, and at times domineering,
Johnston exercised firm control of the mission's
course in fulfilling what he assumed to be its divine
mandate.

By 1975 TEAM could point to major accomplishments
in France. Most significant were the twelve AEEI
churches, five of which were under French leadership.
No other mission had established as many churches, and
no other mission church could rival Orly in size.
TEAM had become a convinced advocate of the church-
growth ideas, especially in its work among the receptive Antillian population in the suburbs south of
Paris. TEAM had lead the long and generally
successful effort to convince American evangelicals
that France was indeed a mission field which demanded
their attention. Of all the missions in France, TEAM
appeared to be the most organized and purposeful.

But the TEAM mission in France suffered from at
least four major weaknesses. Each of these problems
was a direct result of the mission's areas of
strength. Only the next generation would tell whether
the strength would be perennially crippled by the
weakness, or would overcome it.

The first problem stemmed from TEAM's emphasis
upon church planting. On the positive side of TEAM's
diligent work were those twelve churches. But half of
these had fewer than twenty members, and some had
fewer than ten. Had TEAM demonstrated wisdom by identifying each of its groups as a church, thereby draw-
ing the French sympathizers immediately to a local
assembly to which they must be committed? Or had TEAM
deluded itself and its public by denoting these small
groups as churches?

The second problem concerned the future of the
predominately Antillian churches. Would their dramatic growth call attention to evangelical Christianity,
and somehow enable greater penetration of French
society? Or would they serve only to isolate TEAM
from the mainstream of French society in the Parisian
suburbs?

Third, the TEAM churches stuck to strict sectarian policies, and they all belonged to the TEAM-sponsored church association, the Alliance des Eglises Indépendantes. Did the clear-cut policies and large association provide the sense of identity needed for growth? Or had TEAM drawn the wagons in a circle, guarding its niche in France?

Finally, TEAM's success in France owed much to its large investment of funds and personnel. TEAM spent a lot of money in France. Its annual expenditure rose from $14,218 in 1953 to $202,803 in 1975.[34] The total investment for over twenty years was approximately one million dollars. And the mission's accomplishment in that country (perhaps commendable in France, but meager in comparison to other mission fields) occupied the time and energy of thirty-three missionaries by the mid-1970's. Would the AEEI churches in France deveuop as healthy French churches because in their infancy they had received heavy doses of guidance and financial aid from the Americans? Or would they be dependent forever on American money and missionaries? The final verdict on TEAM's mission to France awaited the answers to these questions.

In the last half of the 1960's and in the early 1970's the Greater Europe Mission attempted to revitalize its lagging efforts to establish churches by using "short-term missonaries", usually American young people to provide extra hands for summer construction projects as well as for literature evangelism. The Greater Europe Mission was not the only mission to use short-term missionaries, and the practice brought problems as well as help.[35] On the positive side, the short-term missionary programs gave first-hand experience in missions to a number of young Americans. It was hoped that in some an interest in a missionary career would be quickened. In any case, the program served to make missionary work more widely known in America. On the other hand, there was some opposition to the new practice. Some older missionaries claimed that anyone unable to make a lifetime commitment had not been called to missions.[36] Others wondered if the missionaries' progress in cultural adaptation were not hindered by the arrival each summer of young volunteers who spoke no French. A group of bright-eyed, energetic American teenagers, anxious to "help", could demand more work than they provided. And might not the French, even the French evangelicals, wonder if the short-term missionaries were really long-term tourists? Nonetheless, in spite of these problems, the need for extra hands encouraged more missions to turn to short-term help. However, this led to no major change in the Greater Europe Mission's frustrated attempts to achieve church growth and church planting in northern France.

The slow progress of evangelism did not diminish the accomplishments of the mission's European Bible Institute in Lamorlaye. Developing along the lines laid down in the 1950's, the European Bible Institute continued to expand in size and impact. The number of students continued a slow but steady climb, from forty-three in 1961 to seventy in 1975. The growth in the number of students stood in sharp contrast to the decline in the number of graduates of the French Protestant Reformed seminaries in Paris and Montpellier.[37] This was a critical distinction for the evangelical missionaries in France. Although their progress was slow, at least it was progress. Most instititional Christianity in secular France continued to wither.

The Bible Institute was the seminal idea of the Greater Europe Mission, and the most important aspect of its mission in France. In 1975 the basic philosophy of the institute was still the same ideal which had motiviated the founder Robert Evans in 1948: the most lasting contribution which American missionaries could make in France was not the establishment of their own churches and organizations, but the training of Frenchmen who could accomplish those tasks better than foreigners. Of the nearly four hundred graduates, over 90% took positions in full-time Christian service as pastors, evangelists, missionaries, and teachers.[38]

Nothwithstanding its success, the European Bible Institute had its critics. From outside the confines of evangelical circles there came the expected French criticism that no American missionary effort was needed in France. This was an attitude which confronted all evangelical work, in France and elsewhere, and was not a source of concern to the missionaries. But there was also criticism from within the evangelical fold, even after the initial suspicion and hostility of the French evangelical community had been overcome. First, it was said that the European Bible Institute did not accomplish the task it advertised:

126

"Training Europeans to Evangelize Greater Europe."
This charge stemmed from the significant number of
graduates, as high as 15% or 20%, who became
missionaries to other countries rather than staying in
Europe. Convinced that France needed Christian
workers more than did Africa, a number of French
evangelicals and American missionaries in France
lamented the loss of scarce trained personnel. This
strange phenomenon was not unique to the school at
Lamorlaye. Other European evangelical institutions
such as Nogent Bible Institute in suburban Paris and
Emmaus Bible Institute in French Switzerland witnessed
a similar overseas drain of their graduates.
Therefore, the phenomenon was not caused by the
Americans. This may have brought some comfort to the
missionaries at the European Bible Institute, but it
did not increase the number of evangelical workers in
France. However, the mid-1970's saw slow gains in the
percentage of French graduates who remained in France.
Some who initially had gone to Africa decided to
return to France where they saw a greater need for
their services.

The other major criticism was that the Greater
Europe Mission had put the cart before the horse by
expecting Bible school graduates to start churches.
These observers maintained that the American missionary emphasis should have been placed initially on the
establishment of churches, and then secondly on the
creation of Bible schools. The small number of evangelical churches in France, it was felt, kept small
the pool from which students were drawn. If the
churches existed first, they would have sent to the
Bible institute their young people who were interested
in Christian work. Furthermore, the churches would
have provided the opportunities for employment in the
ministry which the Bible institute graduates needed.
Those who held this view pointed to the Bible schools
of the United States which were developed to support
and preserve those evangelical churches which were
already in existence.

Evans was aware of this alternative, but he
remained convinced of the basic philosophy of the
school. The analogy drawn to the relationship between
Bible schools and churches in America, he felt, was
particularly inappropriate in its application to the
situation in France. He agreed that nothing would
have been of greater aid to his mission's school than
a large number of evangelical churches from which to

receive students and to which to send pastors. But
Evans maintained that when the establishment of
churches necessitated crossing cultural lines, it was
far better to train Frenchmen to establish French
churches than to rely upon an intensive effort by
American missionary church planters who would sometime
turn the work over to the French with the concomitant
withdrawal pains.[39]. However, the number of
institute graduates who devoted themselves to starting
new churches remained small. Perhaps this reflected
the composition of the student body. About half were
recent converts. This often made them bold evangelists, but it meant that they had acquired little
concept of the role of the local church.

Of the American evangelical missions in France,
the Greater Europe Mission shared with TEAM the position of preeminence in influence and size. The ultimate goal for each was the same: working themselves
out of a job through the establishment of a strong
evangelical Christianity in a secular or de-Christianized France. The two missions differed on strategy:
TEAM directed its efforts into church planting, while
the primary focus of the Great Europe Mission was the
European Bible Institute. Yet the Greater Europe
Mission began a church planting effort in Amiens and
other cities of northern France. And TEAM maintained
a continuing interest in evangelical education through
its close relationship with Nogent and its active role
in the establishment of the seminary at Vaux-sur-
Seine. The Greater Europe Mission, like TEAM, at
first projected a heavy (some would say heavy-handed)
American impression. American determination to succeed, coupled with French cultural sensitivity (some
would say touchiness) resulted in some hard feelings.
But the Americans became more sophisticated in their
adaptation to French culture, and the French evangelicals more appreciative of the American contribution.
The school at Chatou and then at Lamorlaye, at first a
source of contention, eventually did much to bring the
two together.

Leadership was as important in the Greater Europe
Mission as it was in TEAM. The mission was not a one-
man show, but the organization reflected the beliefs
and personality of its founder, Robert Evans. His was
not the energetic, driving, day-by-day administration
with which Johnston led TEAM. The Greater Europe
Mission had more than its share of administrative
problems. The mission suffered a relatively high rate

128

of personnel loss, some of which was attributed to administrative problems both within Europe and between the missionaries and the board in America. Administration and attention to detail were not Evans' forte. Furthermore, his direct influence on the missionaries in France lessened as he spent lengthy periods away from France, supervising the expansion of Greater Europe Mission throughout Europe. Evans' leadership of the Greater Europe Mission was through his vision, not his supervision. He was convinced of a divine calling to his missionary task in Europe, and he was the dominant figure in the American missionary work in France. The ideas and goals which spurred the young ex-chaplain to action in the late 1940's were then termed either unnecessary, unpractical, or impossible. But one by one each of the objectives which Evans had outlined in the charter of the Ligue Biblique Francaise at the beginning of his work came to fruition. In his book, his mission, and his institute -- each with its strengths and weaknesses -- Evans projected the image of American missions in France.

In 1975 the American evangelical missionary movement in postwar France passed a significant milestone when it entered its second generation. The ranks of the more than 300 American missionaries in France included for the first time a few grown children of some of the older missionaries. Mission strategists who once planned the whirlwind evangelization of France in the 1940's, now thought in terms of generations. The missionaries marched to a slow drummer. Their story held much failure, more failure than success. For every receptive discussion on a French threshold there were hundreds of slammed doors and rude replies. For every letter of inquiry there were thousands of pieces of Christian literature which ended in the waste basket. Plans were thwarted and strategies fizzled. After much counselling French people professed conversion, only to fall away later. Thousands of "promising contacts" led nowhere. But persistent failures seemed to make accomplishments all the more important. Although at times meager, the accomplishments described in the preceding pages were celebrated by the missionaries as successful, even miraculous, achievements within a culture which proved to be highly resistant to the fulfillment of their objectives. Being more easily discerned, accomplishments received more attention than failures. Most histories concern themselves with what happened, rather than with what failed to happen. But in this case it is crucial to remember that much of the story of what happened in the course of missionary activity in France lies in what failed to happen. Discouragement and failure became common, success a rare pleasure.

Perhaps to some extent this is true of all human endeavor. Certainly it is true in all missionary work. Traditionally, Christian missionaries assumed that in most cases only a few would prove receptive to their message, most would be indifferent, and some would be hostile. But few societies in modern times proved more impervious to evangelical missionaries than France. The missionaries were aware of this, but they did not know why. There was no general agreement on whether their failure to penetrate French society was due to theological, personal, sociological, or methodological reasons. And yet they felt a compelling need to find the answer. They wanted to isolate the problems, solve them, and become successful in their mission to France. They also felt obliged to explain their failures to the people back in American who sent them and supported them. The key to it all lay somewhere in the relationship between American attitudes, evangelical doctrine, and French society.

CHAPTER V NOTES

[1]McGavran, Understanding Church Growth, p. 49. See also McQuilken, Measuring the Church Growth Movement (Chicago: Moody Press, 1973); B. Wilson, "Religion and Churches in Contemporary America," in McLoughlin and Bellah, eds., p. 101.

[2]Church Growth Bulletin, Institute For Church Growth, S. Pasadena, Vol. IX, no. 6, p. 334.

[3]James Burroughs, newsletter, CBFMS, n.d.

[4]1966 Annual Report; Randall Mathews, newsletter, n.d., CBFMS.

[5]1969 Annual Report, 1970 Annual Report, CBFMS.

[6]David Dixon, newsletter, October 11, 1971, CBFMS.

[7]Mehl, p. 275.

[8]J. Beaujeu-Garnier, La Population Francaise (Paris: Librairie Armand Colin, 1969), pp. 104, 129, 130, 155, 161.

[9]Beaujeu-Garnier, p. 85; Jean Francois Six, Cheminements de la Mission de France 1941-1966 (Paris: Editions de Seuil), p. 226.

[10]Pin-Carrier, Essais de Sociologie religieuse (Paris: Spes, 1967); G. Le Bras, Etudes de Sociologie Religieuse (Paris: Universitaires de France, 1955); Boulard, An Introduction to Religious Sociology, tr. R. J. Jackson, (London: Darton, Longman and Todd, 1960), pp. XXV, 3-7, 15, 48-51, 74-85.

[11]Annual Reports, 1975-81, CBFMS; H. Collins, newsletter, August, 1975; letter from M. Bittner, CBFMS, June, 1976.

[12]John Mitchell, newsletters, July, 1968, October, 1968, May, 1970, Evangelical Baptist Missions, Hawthorne, New Jersey; Wilbur Barnes, newsletter, April, 1972, Evangelical Baptist Missions.

[13]Alan Bonnelle, Newsletters, September, 1956, April, 1957, April, 1958, European Evangelistic Crusade.

[14]France Report, 1975, WEF.

[15]Claude Brunel, "Jesus contre la drogue," Lecture pour tous, No. 217 (Fev. 1972), pp. 16-25; Stotts, p. 256; New York Times, September 24, 1966, p. 24.

[16]Stotts, pp. 205, 225, 297..

[17]Jesse Stalley, No Frontiers (London: Burlington Press, n.d.); Congress on World Evangelization (Lausanne, 1974), p. 2.

[18]Phillip Hallie, Lest Innocent Blood Be Shed (New York: Harper, 1979).

[19]William Adams, "Church Planting with a French Pastor," report given at 1972 Foreign Workers Conference; The Gospel Message, Winter, 1970; Fall, 1979, Gospel Missionary Union; 1976 Annual Report, Gospel Missionary Union.

[20]Thomas Julien, 1972 Report, National Fellowship of Brethren Churches, Foreign Missions.

[21]T. Julien, newsletter, summer, 1976. NFBC.

[22]Lifeline, Fourth Quarter, 1964, Unevangelized Fields Mission.

[23]Annual Reports, 1971-1975, UFM.

[24]Annual Reports, 1972-1975, UFM.

[25]See J. Ardagh, The New French Revolution (New York: Harper and Row, 1968), p. 122-128.

[26]Annual Program, 1965-1966, TEAM.

[27]1965 Annual Conference Report, p. 31, TEAM.

[28]Sheetz, p. 198; Annual Conference Reports, 1967, 1968, 1969; letter from Arthur Johnston to Vernon Mortenson, August 18, 1969, TEAM.

[29]Tom Harris, "Working with the 'Antillais' in Light of Their Responsiveness," paper read at SemiAnnual Conference, February 27, 1973.

[30]Letters from Gay Harris, missionary in Créteil, to the author, March 13, 1973, April 15, 1976; Field Chairman's Report, 1975, TEAM.

[31]1967 Annual Conference Report, TEAM, p. 19.

[32]Letters, Arthur Johnston to Vernon Mortenson, April 8, 1964, April 16, 1964, TEAM.

[33]France Executive Committee Minutes, August 22, 1968, Conservative Baptist Foreign Mission Society; G. Dagon, ed., Petites Eglises de France, 5 vols. (Saverne: Imprimerie Savernoise, 1966-73), fails to list AEEI churches.

[34]Annual Report, 1977 Field Conference, TEAM, p. A-1.

[35]Meredith Long, "The Increasing Role of Short-Term Service in Today's Missions," Mission Handbook: North American Protestant Ministries Overseas (Monrovia, CA: Missions Advanced Research and Communication Center, 1979), pp. 16-23.

[36]J. Kane, Winds of Change in the Christian Mission (Chicago: Moody Press, 1973), pp. 140-145.

[37]Letter from C. Preuss, Librarian, Faculté de Théologie Protestante, Montpellier, to the author, August 10, 1974; letter from J. Fisher, Secretary, Institute Faculté Protestante de Theologie, Paris, to the author, April 26, 1974.

[38]Reporter, Summer, 1969, GEM, p. 2; European Bible Institute Report 1965, GEM; European Bible Institute, newsletter, June, 1976, GEM.

[39]See Brian Jones in the Evangelical Missions Quarterly, Spring, 1972, p. 142.

CHAPTER VI

THE AMERICAN MISSIONARIES IN FRENCH SOCIETY

The activity of American evangelical missionaries in France in the postwar era focused on one basic theme: their effectual communication of the gospel in a foreign culture. They were less successful in this than they had hoped, so they tried to discover the basic cause of their discouraging failure.

Some thought the reasons might be spiritual: perhaps God had simply not chosen to bestow His grace upon modern France. Or, perhaps consequently, France was too much under the influence of the devil. Or, a missionary's failure might be traced to inadequacies in his own relationship with God.

But while all missionaries affirmed that nothing could be accomplished without the blessing of God, few were content to conclude their examination of their own under-achievement with a personal opinion that the timing of divine dispensation. Instead, the missionaries turned their attention to the special problem which French culture raised for evangelical Christianity.

Some missionaries, and many French evangelicals, believed that the postwar missionary effort would have been successful if the Americans had properly adapted themselves to French culture, and if they had striven for assimilation into French society. These individuals were convinced that the failure of the French to respond to the missionaries was due to the missionaries' distinctive and often offensive American behavior. A larger faction of missionaries claimed that no matter how much the missionaries attempted to conform to French culture, the response would still be negative. This group viewed culture through the prism of their evangelical doctrine. The problem, they said, lay in French culture itself. They concluded that there were basic incompatibilities between evangelical Christianity and French culture, and that Frenchmen could become true Christians only if they renounced certain French values and customs.

But whether the missionary was primarily attempting to change the society or conform to it, some degree of adaptation was necessary. There were some missionaries who made little attempt to understand the

French, much less to conform to their customs. Complaining about the unavailability of peanut butter and corn on the cob, or defiantly reading Time magazine in language class, these missionaries did not stay in France for more than one term. But often that would be long enough for them to discredit the other missionaries who were making a genuine effort to adapt to French culture. Some tried too hard, and sought French acceptance by renouncing and attacking anything American. These two extreme forms of behavior were common manifestations of culture shock. Immersion into a foreign culture could be a trying and even traumatic experience. Most mission agencies realized this, and attempted to prepare missionary candidates for the problems of enculturation. But they normally focused upon the primitive cultures to which missionaries were traditionally sent. Many of the missionaries bound for France assumed they would have little trouble with the new culture. After all, they faced no tribal initiations, and they could enjoy indoor plumbing, television, supermarkets, and Coca Cola. But the superficial similarities in brand names and modern gadgets hid the chasm which separated French and American life.

Little things meant a lot. The cumulative effect of a thousand and one small differences in table etiquette, dress customs, shopping procedures, social protocol, and thought patterns led to the tension and anxiety of culture shock. Even the most broad-minded and well-intentioned Americans felt frustrated and confused without all the familiar social cues which oriented them in the situations of daily life.[1] Some missionaries never moved beyond the two self-centered and opposite reactions to culture shock. They either attempted frantically to "go native", or they clung blindly and immovably to American ways.[2] Most of the missionaries at least attempted to move beyond the initial culture shock toward empathy and identification with the French people. Successful adaptation to a new culture required , above all, adjustments to the people's expectations. Sometimes the Americans, as foreigners, were expected to do things differently. Other times they were not. Knowing which time was which was the problem. The American missionaries in France varied widely in both their success in cultural adaptation and in their perception of their success.

The language was a big hurdle. Almost all the missionaries labored under a linguistic handicap. Very few had received any training in French before arriving in France.[3] American missionaries rarely achieved a degree of fluency acceptable to the average Frenchman. More often than not the missionaries, even some who had lived in France for over a decade, spoke with a heavy foreign accent. This did not help them in their task of verbal persuasion among a people who viewed mispronunciation of its language as obnoxious, not quaint. The missions usually did not assign proper priority to acquiring the necessary linguistic proficiency. There were several reasons for this. The chief one was time. Always in need of additional personnel, the missions working in France pressed the new arrivals into full-time work as rapidly as possible, and consequently many mission agencies set aside only two years for language study, while some stipulated one year or less. The training which the new missionaries received at the Alliance Francaise, the Sorbonne, or even in language schools in Quebec was designed to meet only minimal standards. Furthermore, the relatively brief time allotted to language study was often interrupted. This was especially true for missionary wives who often were forced to suspend their language work in order to care properly for their children. But it was not uncommon for the men to be interrupted in language study if the mission needed an extra pair of hands in a building project or in literature distribution.

English was commonly spoken in missionary homes, not only because it was easier than speaking French, but also in order to maintain an American identity for the sake of the children. Few critics of the mission-aries' language preparation attacked this, even though it did retard linguistic facility. However, criticism was directed at the use of English among the adult missionaries, and to the common practice of assigning recent graduates of a language study program to work on projects with several missionaries in which they would all speak English. A few weeks or months of this served to erode some of the achievement of diffi-cult months in language study.

Linguistic aptitude was never the primary consid-eration in the acceptance of missionary candidates by mission boards, and many of them had a difficult and discouraging time in language school. Their first attempts at personal evangelism were frequently described as traumatic. Embarassing moments occurred. One missionary occasionally gave a little talk on joy, and noticed that his listeners always broke into laughter as soon as he suggested that they wear a smile (sourire). Only much later did he realize that instead he had urged them to wear a mouse (souris). Another of these inevitable gaffes involved a missionary speaker who, attempting to say "the angel of God appeared" repeatedly proclaimed, "the laundry of God appeared." For some missionaries the persistent language problem was of such magnitude that it brought about a personality change. Bold effervescence gave way to reserved timidity. Conceptual thoughts of educated minds could find expression only in shallow conversation. Veteran missionaries were bothered by linguistic inadequacies even after as much as fifteen or twenty years in France, and they frequently expressed the opinion that an additional year of language study would have been worth the time.[1] Mission leaders gradually dealt with the language problem by tightening the requirements, but more often merely by reminding the new missionaries that a Christian character exhibiting sincere love for the French people should cover a multitude of grammatical sins.[2] Another communication problem stemmed from the missionaries' unsure grasp of French thought forms, especially in the area of religious ideas. French audiences accustomed to Cartesian logic and carefully framed arguments were not swayed by pre-digested American evangelistic sermons in which fundamentalist American theologians, unknown to the French, were cited as authorities.[6] This persistent weakness in communication crippled their efforts to function smoothly in French society.

In spite of their desire to achieve identity with their French neighbors, the missionaries preserved much of their American culture. Few missionaries found themselves alone in French society. Most worked with fellow Americans at least every other day. Missions which grouped their personnel in one area, like Paris, Grenoble, or Bordeaux, commonly held weekly or monthly meetings. This sustained their American ways and image. The larger pattern of American life was preserved when missionaries arranged Halloween parties for their children, met for Thanksgiving dinner, and celebrated the Fourth of July.[7] A few American customs helped their work. Occasionally hamburger cookouts, barbecues, and even Tupperware parties proved to be novelties which attracted French guests. Some of the very few missionary contacts with the French upper class came at these patently American affairs.[8] Some missionaries decided that it was unnecessary or too difficult to adopt the daily schedule of French living, so they stuck to American eating habits and work hours. Missionaries in the Paris region frequented American-style shops, and checked into the American hospital for medical care.[9] Pride in America and in the American way of doing things was difficult to forsake, and many missionaries found it impossible to remain silent when their homeland was criticized by the French.

Missionary homes looked more American than French. Economic considerations usually compelled Americans to take to France their appliances and furniture. Although this issue was not a major factor in the process of acclimitization to French culture, it was another small obstacle to assimilation. In the early years of the missionary presence in France the mere possession of appliances and automobiles raised an economic barrier in addition to the cultural one. The foreign flavor of the missionary endeavor also persisted from the names of the missionary organizations, and perhaps unavoidably from the names of the missionaries themselves.

If cultural orientation can be discerned by reading preference, the missionaries were very much American. Although a handful professed to be well-read in French literature, most did little secular reading other than keeping up with current events. Although all tuned in regularly to French radio or television, most relied upon American periodicals as their source for news. Several depended primarily upon radio broadcasts of the Voice of America or the British Broadcasting Corporation. Few were regular readers of French newspapers; the cost of subscription was often cited as prohibitive. Reading taste was uniform: <u>Time</u>, <u>Reader's Digest</u>, <u>The National Geographic</u>, <u>Christianity Today</u>, <u>Moody Monthly</u>, and <u>Eternity</u> lay around the average missionary home.

In many ways, the missionaries responded to the differences between their homeland and France like other foreigners living in France. They all experienced difficulty in adapting to the language, the French ethic of the road, the confusion of daily shopping, and the balky telephone system. The missionaries were poorly prepared, but no worse than the

average American businessman transferred to serve a
stint in the Paris office.[10]. Successful cultural
adjustment depended upon personal preference for the
French way of life and personal determination to
modify or abandon American attitudes. A few missionaries claimed they had become thoroughly French in
outlook and behavior; others said they lived in two
cultures, no longer fully at home in either; but most,
although feeling content and even accepted in France,
remained very much American. Continually trying to
adjust to a foreign culture produced continual emotional stress within many of the Americans. Although
committed to their work in France, they frequently
yearned for home.

The missionaries displayed considerable differences in their perception of their own success in
bridging the cultural gap. Some exhibited a superficial understanding of the problem, confidently pro-
claiming that they had bridged the gap merely because
they had been invited into several French homes.
Another claimed to have become "completely French"
except for his abstinence from wine and coffee, dependence upon American news and sports periodicals, and
maintenance of American eating schedules. Other
missionaries, some of whom had been in France for
twenty years or more, confessed that they never could
become completely French. One culturally sensitive
veteran missionary said that after the initial
cultural shock was over, missionary confidence in
becoming French was inversely proportional to the
years spent in France.

Some of their difficulties were of their own
making. American evangelical taboos, especially concerning alcohol, caused a big problem. The fundamentalist and separatist missionaries did not even debate
the issue of whether or not to drink wine. They cate-
gorically refused it, even when offered by French
hosts. Some missions placed all their personnel under
a pledge of total abstinence, and called upon their
French converts to adopt a similar stance. Many
missionaries made such an agreement before leaving the
United States, but then attempted to modify the policy
once they realized how important wine was to French
social intercourse. If permission to change the
policy was denied, it was often for economic reasons.
Although mission executives admitted that French evangelicals saw nothing amiss in drinking wine, they
feared that American supporters of the mission would

be deeply offended to learn that their missionaries were drinking wine.

Some missions avoided the problem by continually postponing the adoption of a specific policy, allowing individual missionaries to follow the dictates of their consciences, and to accept wine in French homes if they felt it would aid their social acceptance. Although seemingly tangential to the basic missionary purpose in France, the issue of alcohol was a persistent problem, and filled a disproportionate amount of space in the correspondence between the missionaries and their United States headquarters. The French could not readily understand this tempest in a wine glass, and were even more perplexed by the taboos which some missionaires placed upon the movies and dancing.

Successful adaptation to French culture was especially important to the group of missionaries who were convinced that their failure to realize success in their ultimate purpose in France -- the evangelization of the French people -- was due to their failure to adapt successfully to French culture. Consequently, they strove to act and think as much like their French neighbors as possible. If their efforts in evangelism or church planting were still not successful, the missionaries blamed their insufficient progress toward becoming identified with France and its society.

These missionaries pointed to the American style of living maintained by many of their colleagues and to the distinctively American image of some missionary-founded churches with their frothy American gospel choruses. They were certain that most of the missionaries were perceived by their neighbors primarily as Americans, rather than as evangelicals or Protestants. Several missionary pastors admitted that their church was referred to as "the American church," rather than the evangelical church. The missionaries who sought evangelistic success through more complete cultural assimilation objected strenously to what they deemed unnecessary and even foolish insistence that French converts follow American fundamentalist standards of personal and social behavior. It was difficult enough for a Frenchman to embrace the basic tenets of evangelical Christianity without confusing the issue with the encrustations of American evangelical traditions. The evangelization of France was not going to be achieved by turning Frenchmen into Americans.

On the other side of the debate stood a group of missionaries who were equally convinced that the missionary task in France would not be accomplished by turning Americans into Frenchmen. As one unproductive year followed another, an increasing number of missionaries, including several experienced mission leaders, concluded that the primary problem lay not in the difference between American and French cultures, but in the differences which they saw between French culture and the doctrines of evangelical Christianity.

This faction argued that if success could be achieved by assimilation into French culture, why were the French evangelicals so unsuccessful? Their miniscule size and influence demonstrated that merely being French did not guarantee a successful evangelical ministry. The conclusions that French culture was peculiarly resistant to the message of evangelical Christianity was sobering because it required Frenchmen to detach themselves to some extent from their own culture in order to grasp evangelical Christianity. This reversed the usual sequence. Evangelical missionaries maintained that all cultures contained elements contradictory to Christianity, but they expected individuals to convert, and then subsequently renounce those aspects of their culture which were incompatible with their new faith.[11]

For most of their history Christian missions have called people to substantial cultural change as well as a new religion. On traditional mission fields the cultural change was made easier because the missionaries also brought technological, medical and educational progress. The French sought none of these amenities from the American missionaries. Instead, many missionaries concluded, the French maintained patterns of culture which precluded believing or even understanding the evangelical gospel.

The primary problem was the French attitude toward religion. The violent history of religion in France did not produce a very flattering picture of church life. The French had their fill of religion, and pointedly informed the missionaries that they had no interest in it. At the same time, the French professed to know all about religion. The missionaries found that it was very difficult for a Frenchman to believe that he did not understand the evangelical message. In an article in a major American evangelical periodical, a missionary spokesman explained, "The French people, almost to a man, are convinced that they know all about Christianity . . . they think they know the gospel -- that is why the evangelization of France is so difficult."[12]

While the religious attitudes of the French were of little help to the missionary endeavors, the secular and rationalist side of the French mind posed an even greater problem.[13] The zeal for clear thought and expression ("Ce qui n'est pas clair n'est pas francais!") limited the appeal of missionaries who stressed faith, emotion, and too often spoke in translated American cliches. Salvation had little appeal for people who believed they were already free and spiritually autonomous.[14]

Above all, the missionaries lamented the absence of a strong evangelical tradition in French culture. This was not their most clearly reasoned position. Most Christian missionaries did not expect to discover Christian traditions among the people to whom they were sent. Since the Americans in France usually assumed the role of "pioneer" missionaries, they should not have expected to find an evangelical heritage. On the other hand, if they expected France to be more Christian, they should have drawn closer to the Christians already there. They could not have it both ways.

The missionaries were surprised by the French unfamiliarity with the Bible. They often needed to convince Frenchmen that the Bible had not been written by the Protestants. Missionary files abound with references to Frenchmen who had never heard of the Bible, and letters from mayors, teachers, and even nuns who had received their first Bible by responding to a missionary brochure.[15] Encounters with people who had never heard of Jesus Christ were not uncommon. Without an evangelical frame of reference it was often difficult for the French to understand what the missionaries were attempting to do. Even the word evangélique by which the missionaries denoted their work was not readily understood. Frenchmen were confused if not insulted to be approached by a "missionary," so the missionaries learned rather quickly to refer to themselves as pastors rather than missionaries. But this did not always help. In some communities a pastor was afforded a measure of respect, but the French were suspicious of foreign pastors, especially if they had no church. Coming from backgrounds in which the clergy was held in honor, the missionaries were slow to understand the depth of anticlericalism in France. Missionaries said that Frenchmen were puzzled by their decision to leave America in order to live a comparatively meager existence in France. They wanted to know why the missionaries had no job, and why, as Americans, they were starting French churches.

French ignorance of evangelical Christianity rarely changed to curiosity when the missionaries confronted Frenchmen with its basic assertions. Instead, indifference prevailed as the common response. While there were cases of overt and covert opposition to the missionary activity in France, the missionaries were far more disturbed by the indifference with which most Frenchmen met their efforts. Even the few who showed interest normally declined to make a definite commitment. The common expression je ne voudrais pas m'engager terminated many evangelistic discussions.[16] There was an even greater tendency to shrink from a public declaration of faith. Even French evangelicals looked sceptically at the practice of some missionaries to conclude every church service with an altar call or another form of invitation to make a public profession of faith.[17]

The missionaries who stressed the basic incompatibility between French culture and evangelical Christianity mentioned certain traits of French "national character" as particular obstacles to the expansion of evangelical Christianity. French morality, or lack of it, was a theme of missionary newsletters, literature, and reports. The missionaries professed shock at the prevalence of dishonesty which they perceived in French attitudes toward taxation and other civic responsibilities. Another French characteristic which the missionaries criticized was the emphasis on individualism. The Americans, accustomed to teamwork and an ethic which fostered individual sacrifice for group success, were discouraged by the unwillingness of many Frenchmen to relinquish their individual interests for the sake of the group.[18] A discussion about where the church youth group should go on an outing could easily result in an impasse, as four or five options would be presented with no one willing to compromise.

144

A local church was envisioned as a unified body composed of many parts working in harmony, but missionaries often despaired of welding together a church of Frenchmen each bent upon fulfilling his own sense of individualism.

The pattern of life in modern France presented its unique impediments to missionary progress. The pressures and pleasures of urban life seemed to allow no time for religion, and reduced missionary schedules to shambles. Long hours spent commuting, late dinners and television made evening visitation and meetings inconvenient if not impossible. Since the economic pressures of modern France often required both husband and wife to work, door-to-door evangelism by the missionaries often found no one at home. Fatigue and family gatherings filled Sundays with sleeping and eating, with little time for church activities. The growing weekend exodus to the countryside made for even emptier pews.[19] The logistical problems created by the rhythm of French life caused many missionaries to doubt if evangelical Christianity could fit into the schedule.

The social structure of France, while not as great an obstacle in the minds of the missionaries as some of the aspects of French culture just mentioned, was nevertheless a source of confusion and frustration. French family ties impeded evangelism, especially in terms of the vigilantly guarded privacy of the home and the insular position of the family in French society. A rigid class structure limited personal contacts, restricted group dynamics, and denied overtures to the working class as well as the influential haute bourgeoisie.

The missionaries in France, like missionaries everywhere, tried to be agents of social change. But while they had been exposed to facets of French culture, they often failed to understand the functional inter-relationships between them. Socio-cultural change had to be accomplished through individuals, but the missionaries usually concentrated upon individuals who had little capacity to accelerate the desired change in French society. Their extensive involvement with women and children might have added numbers to evangelical groups, but did little to advance the cause of evangelical Christianity in French society. It might have even hindered it. Continuing identification of the missionary movement with people who were

145

not socially innovative or influential invited not only the indifference of the socially influential, but also their censure.[20]

The missionaries who blamed French culture itself for their consistent failure finally pointed to the refreshing success they enjoyed with non-French people. From the earliest days after the war, the groups formed by missionaries contained Italians, Spaniards, Portuguese, Africans, and Antillians who were living in France. In many cases the most active members of missionary churches in France were not Frenchmen.

The missionaries' status in French society determined the success of their efforts. Their identity was as important as their ideology. People wanted to know who they were before they listened to what they had to say. Although the missionaries could not control the way in which the French perceived them, they made critical choices about their relationships in French society which gave them their identity. There were five groups with whom it was possible for the missionaries to have been associated: the Americans, the sects, the Catholics, the Protestants, and the independent evangelicals.

Unfortunately for the missionaries, they were most frequently given the labels they hoped to avoid. All too often they were grouped with the Americans or the sects. This discouraged the missionaries because they sought to establish their relationships on the basis of religious doctrine. The only American relationships they formed were with the members of the American diplomatic, miliary, and business community who shared their evangelical precepts. The missionaries viewed non-evangelical Americans in the same manner as they viewed non-evangelical Frenchmen. Preachers from TEAM, for instance, saw no difference between the weekly evangelistic service in French at the Orly airport and the one held in English at the nearby American airbase. Missionary work presumed that common religious doctrine was sufficient to bridge the gap of national difference. Conversely, the missionaries' attitude toward other Americans in France showed that common nationality was insufficient to bridge the gap of doctrinal difference.

Being classified as one of the sects like the Jehovah's Witnesses or the Mormons bothered the missionaries more than being seen merely as Americans. They regarded the sects as dangerous religious opponents who shared no evangelical doctrines. But they found that the average Frenchman lacked the inclination or the ability to discern the theological differences between the people who came to his door and stuffed his mailbox. The missionaries frequently reported that one of the major difficulties of door-to-door evangelism was the initial necessity to explain that they were not Mormons or Jehovah's Witnesses. The American missionaries were not the only group to suffer this confused identity. Small French denominations like the Baptists, Mennonites, Brethren, and Assemblies of God struggled against similar misperceptions.[21] But the American missionaries encouraged their sect image because they were foreign, they were split into many different groups, and the individual missions had little to do with each other.[22] By 1975 nearly forty American evangelical mission agencies operated in France, with relatively little inter-mission cooperation. Each mission worked busily on its own projects, unaware of what others were doing, much less inclined to find the time to forge a working relationship with another group. But doctrinal issues played a role in inter-mission cooperation, or non-cooperation. Missions with strict ecclesiology policies shied away from those whose statutes might be ambivalent. The separatist missions kept away from the others, and sometimes from each other. Even their cooperative ventures, like a fellowship of premillennial fundamentalist Baptist pastors, seemed sectarian. The sects disturbed the American missionaries, not only because they blurred the missionaries' identity, but also because they often outstripped evangelical growth. Some studies attributed the most rapid religious growth in Europe to the sects, especially among the lower class.[23] Even in thoroughly secularized societies, sects made extensive gains, normally among people resistant to the overtunes of recognized churches.[24] The missionaries thought the growth of the sects pointed to a French desire for religious change, but they were unable to tap it. While their groups appeared too much like sects to most Frenchmen, they looked too much like a church to those drawn to the sects.

The American missionaires tried to avoid not only being identified with the sects, but also being identified with the church which most Frenchmen

recognized, Roman Catholicism. Their doctrinal
beliefs and American evangelical presuppositions kept
them away from the institutions and people which stood
for Christianity in France. American evangelicals
traditionally opposed Roman Catholicism, and the missionaries had their minds made up on this issue before
they arrived in France. From the late 1940's through
the mid-1960's missionary publications and correspondence bristled with statements of doctrinaire opposition to Roman Catholicism. People were cautioned
"never to confuse true evangelical Christianity with
Catholicism" because of its emphasis upon the Virgin
Mary, ritual, and salvation by sacrament or work,
rather than by faith.[25] However, although the
missionaries offered Catholic opposition as a reason
for their slow progress, it was difficult to substan-
tiate a direct correlation between opposition and
failure or, on the other hand, between no opposition
and success.

The missionaries' rigid hostility toward Catholics began to give way when they realized that most
French people made little more than a nominal commitment to the Catholic church. By the early 1960's
missionaries became concerned less about the doctrines
and power of Rome and more about using the French dis-
satisfaction with Catholicism as an opportunity for
evangelism.[30] Then, the Second Vatican Council
caused significant changes in the religious atmosphere, and enabled new contact between the missionaries and Catholicism. Several missionaries worked in
cooperation with the local priest in Christian literature distribution and other evangelistic endeavors.
The Vatican's encouragement of individual Bible reading swelled the numbers attending missionary Bible
studies. The effects of the new charismatic movement
within French Catholicism led veteran missionaries to
call attention to the possibility of an evangelical
revival springing from a rapidly changing French
Catholic community.[31] By 1970 the changes in
Catholicism which followed the Second Vatican Council
had brought about a sigificant change in the established evangelical attitude. Wary overtures and hopeful but limited cooperation replaced the rigid
hostility of earlier years.

But the American missionary community was not
about to initiate a rapprochement with Catholicism.
The optimism generated by the results of Vatican II
could not overcome strong suspicion. Some

148

fundamentalist missionaries dismissed the changed
Catholicism as merely another manifestation of the
loathed ecumenical movement, and hence avoided all
contact with it.[32] Other missions attempted evangelistic methods which capitalized on the new Catholic
climate, but carefully refused any cooperative gesture
which might identify the mission with a Catholic
church, project, or publishing house.[33] TEAM, for
instance, formulated a policy which encouraged missionaries to engage Roman Catholics in evangelistic
discussions and Bible study, but called upon them to
maintain the traditional evangelical separation from
Roman Catholicism because Catholics still did not subscribe to the fundamental evangelical doctrine of the
authority of Scripture. The missionaries sought converts within the framework of the new dialogue between
Protestants and Catholics, but their efforts, even
when successful, sometimes did not produce the desired
results. Those who were disenchanted enough with
Catholicism to join an evangelical church often
brought along their minimalist attitude toward church
participation.[34] Others responded to missionary
Bible teaching with a renewed zeal for the Catholic
church.[35] French Catholics readily criticized
their church, but were reluctant to leave it. Nonetheless, the missionaries continued to press their
converts to sever promptly and completely their connection with Catholicism because of doctrinal differences. A few missionaries wished to modify this firm
stance so they could cooperate with French Catholics
who were concerned about their de-Christianized
nation. Others sought to find ways for new evangelicals to remain in the Catholic church. These attitudes usually drew swift rebuke from other
missionaries.[36] Staunchly insisting upon
doctrinal precision, and firmly controlled by traditional American evangelical sentiment, the missionaries in France maintained their distance from the
Roman Catholic church even though some admitted that
demanding converts to renounce Catholic culture and
traditions would keep evangelical numbers in France
perennially small.

The doctrinal positions and evangelical traditions which kept the missionaries away from Catholics
also barred them from a relationship with most French
Protestants. The strange tendency of the missionaries
to ignore their fellow Protestants, including the
50,000 evangelical Christians in the Reformed and
Lutheran churches has already been discussed. The

149

American evangelical movement shunned the mainline
Protestant denominations, accusing their seminaries
and pastors of having abandoned the Bible in favor of
liberal theological novelties. Evangelicals from
small denominations also looked askance at the modern
ecumenical movement, branding it a subtle, even
Satanic, scheme for compromising and watering-down
Biblical doctrine in the name of unity. The missionaries harbored these religious and cultural attitudes
long before they left America, and wrote off the major
French denominations, especially the French Reformed
Church, before they arrived. This step, premature and
perhaps avoidable, eliminated the best solution to
their identity problem.

However, within French Protestantism, the small
minority of independent evangelicals, mainly Baptists
and Brethren, shared the missionaries' basic beliefs.
Like the missionaries, these people kept out of the
mainstream of French Protestantism. The Annuaire
Evangélique, a directory of evangelical churches and
pastors, neglected entirely the Reformed and Lutheran
churches; similarly the Protestant Federations' La
France Protestant Annuaire excluded the Brethren, most
missionary-founded churches, and the Assemblies of
God.

Doctrinal affinity brought the American missionaries and the French evangelicals together, but they
had their differences and even disputes. More often
than not the French termed the differences cultural,
while the Americans claimed that they were doctrinal.
Intially, economic differences grated upon French
sensitivity and sparked friction between the Americans
and the French evangelicals. The frosty reception
given by the French evangelicals to some early
missionary attempts with their American methods,
lavish budgets, and new cars has already been mentioned. Differences in education and experience posed
problems for immediate cooperation between the French
and American evangelicals. The Europeans felt that
the Americans were naive and culturally unsophisti-
cated, while the Americans claimed that the French
were parochial and out of touch with evangelical
affairs in other parts of France and throughout the
world.

Other small problems stemmed from cultural
differences and sensitive personalities. The French
felt that the Americans could have made a stronger

attempt to learn their language, and could have sought their advice or even approval before starting their work. French evangelicals felt slighted when missionary executives from the States traveled through France, conferring with only the missionaries. French feelings became injured when missionaries said or implied that their service in France was one of personal sacrifice. A few French evangelicals who had been to America confidentially complained that some American missionaries did not work as hard as evangelicals in the United States, and the French wondered if missions attracted second class personnel.[37] The American missionaries, on the other hand, expressed dismay at the bickering and pettiness within the tiny, fragmented French evangelical community.[38] But as the Americans slowly made adaptations to French culture, and as the contacts between the two groups increased, many Americans decided that the differences between them were more doctrinal than cultural.

Evangelism was the issue, and the Americans concluded that the French did not take seriously enough the Biblical passages mandating the proclamation of the gospel. The missionaries asserted unanimously their conclusions that the French evangelicals had little vision for growth and were too content with the status quo or even with the glories of the Huguenot past. The French acknowledged their reluctance to emphasize numbers and growth. Jacques Blocher, often the spokesman for French evangelicals, was found of illustrating the difference in outlook with an anecdote. Referring to a government proposal during the Napoleonic era to give the Protestants in Paris the large Madeleine church, Blocher noted that the offer was refused because the Protestants thought the building too large. "They had no vision," Blocher continued wryly, "because the American missionaries had not yet arrived."[39]

Another example of a doctrinal dispute which became a barrier to cooperation between these two varieties of evangelicals was the debate over premillennialism. This controversy slowed the founding of the evangelical seminary at Vaux-sur-Seine. The American missionaries stressed their conviction that Christ must return before the prophesied millennium, and they insisted this be included in the written statement of faith. The French evangelicals, split into premillennial, postmillennial, and amillennial camps, considered the issue secondary and open to theological debate. After months and even years of fruitless attempts to find common ground on this issue, the seminary opened without an explicit premillennial stance, but with the implicit understanding that premillennial doctrine would be taught.[40] In some cases, doctrinal differences within the Franco-American evangelical camp were sharp enough to preclude cooperation. A few fundamentalist Baptist missionaries even refused all contact with the French Baptist Federation because the latter allegedly contained some liberal pastors and congregations.

Notwithstanding these problems, it would be a distortion to emphasize the differences and disputes between the American missionaries and the French evangelicals. Their cooperation was more important. The French evangelicals formed the one group in France with whom the Americans could identify, and to whom they made sincere attempts to adapt. Specific examples of cooperation in evangelism, literature distribution, and faculty exchanges between Bible schools need not be recounted here. Instead, a discussion of the relationship between the missionaries of TEAM and neighboring French evangelicals will demonstrate the nature and progress of their cooperation.

Geographical proximity encouraged cooperation between the TEAM missionaries working in or near Orly and the French evangelicals at the nearby Nogent Bible Institute. The directors of the institute, Blocher and Nicole, freely offered their assistance to the Americans, and were especially helpful in unraveling bureaucratic snarls encountered in the renting and construction of buildings. They also prodded the Americans toward a greater understanding of French ways of doing things.[41] At the same time, Arthur Johnston accepted gratefully invitations to teach courses at the institute from time to time. Having assured themselves and the Chicago headquarters that the men at Nogent held the same doctrinal views as TEAM,[42] the missionaries sought further cooperation. The Americans aided the French children's camp program, and sent several young men from TEAM's newly founded churches to study at the Nogent institute.

The best example of the cooperation between the Americans and the French was the formation of TEAM's church association, the <u>Alliance des Eglises Evangéliques Indépendantes</u>, or AEEI. French evangelicals from Nogent and elsewhere assisted the Americans by contributing their advice, prestige, and membership. Blocher suggested the organization's name, supplied its statement of faith in French, and became its honorary president.

As their evangelistic efforts in France met with some success, the missionaries found they had to deal with two varieties of French evangelicals. In addition to those present when the missionaries arrived in France, there were the newly converted evangelicals who were the products of the missionary work. All missions claimed that their ultimate goal was the establishment of French evangelical Christianity strong enough to make missionary work in France unnecessary. Therefore they needed to find young French evangelicals with leadership potential whom they could groom for the assumption of major responsibility. This presented the common dilemma between fostering independence and maintaining control.

The relationship between the American mission-aries and the French evangelicals within the AEEI demonstrated a slow shift in the American attitude as the young French evangelicals matured. When the AEEI was founded in 1958 the Americans assured mission control of the organization by filling seventeen of the twenty-five charter memberships.[43] By the mid-1960's a few more Frenchmen had joined the association and some, like Marc Atger and Marc Descheemaecker, worked intimately with the missionaries in their work. The missionaries indicated sincere appreciation of the French contribution, but also insisted that the day of French leadership, although apparently approaching, had not yet arrived.[44] By 1973, however, the mission felt sure enough of Marc Descheemaecker to place him in the presidency of the AEEI. The mission-aries spoke proudly of their progress toward elevating their French co-workers to a position of equal part-nership.[45] But Descheemaecker and other young French members of the AEEI were very much a product of TEAM, cast in an acceptable mold. TEAM depended on the AEEI to preserve its American brand of evangelical doctrines in France, and did not risk losing control of organization and its member churches.

Although the relationship between the American missionaries and the French evangelicals had not achieved complete harmony by 1975 (each annoyed the other from time to time), considerable progress had been made in fostering an evangelical community in France which transcended national differences. The French concerns about American cultural insensitivity became muted as the missionaries attempted to conform to French customs. And the American criticisms of French attitudes toward evangelism were assuaged by new French evangelistic activities including youth rallies and dial-a-prayer programs. When the Americans could convince themselves that differing French attitudes or behavior did not stem from doctrinal differences, cooperation became much easier. The missionaries who made the most progress in achieving cooperation were those who realized that some of their secondary doctrines, such as premillennialism, were shaped as much by their own American evangelical subculture as by orthodox Biblical interpretation.

The Americans gradually realized that the French evangelicals, after all, had been gracious, cordial, and helpful to the uninvited foreign missionaries. After the Americans had experienced frustration and failure in France, they appreciated the difficult task faced by the overworked and poorly supported French evangelical workers. Always pressing the French evangelicals to move forward, by the 1960's the Americans realized how hard they had to work just to stand still.

The French, for their part, recognized that the Americans had made a vital contribution to evangelical Christianity in France, and that their presence, in a culturally acceptable form, was actually needed. The pastor of a well-known French evangelical church in Paris termed the missionary work "considerable and eminently usueful," while other evangelical leaders came to acknowledge their debt to the Americans in church planting and evangelism.[46]

There was one group of French evangelical Christians with whom the missionaries did not enjoy an amicable or working relationship. The French pentecostals, by most estimates, were the fastest growing religious group in France.[47] Their foreign origin, emphasis upon growth and emotion, and evangelical doctrine of salvation by faith gave the pentecostals a large amount of common ground with the American missionaries. But doctrinal differences precluded cooperation or agreement. In spite of their common evangelical soteriology (usually sufficient to serve as a common denominator for cooperation), a deep difference prevailed over the doctrine of the Holy Spirit. The disagreements concerning healing, prophecy, and speaking in tongues created a barrier between the missionaries and the most aggressively evangelistic Christians in France. A few missionaries, especially those who had lost members of their groups to rival Pentecostal assemblies, were openly opposed and even hostile to the French pentecostals. Others were wary of pentecostal proselytizing and generally refused cooperation with them, but maintained a live-and-let-live posture.[48]

The troubled relationship between the American missionaries and the French pentecostals had nothing to do with cultural or national differences. Similar problems existed between the French evangelicals and French pentecostals, as well as between pentecostals and non-pentecostals in the United States. The American missionaries merely maintained the position toward pentecostalism which prevailed in their mission societies and churches at home.

The doctrinal considerations which determined the nature and extent of the relationship the missionaries formed in France also shaped their political attitudes. Their reluctance to make a commitment within the context of French politics paralleled their disinclination to establish a relationship or sense of identity with the major religious groups in France. The missionaries never became involved in questions of national politics, and their relationship with local politicians and bureaucrats was limited to requests for permission to conduct meetings, erect tents and loudspeakers, and to construct buildings. There were a few occasions when a missionary played a Catholic official against a communist in order to gain a permit, but except for the normal frustrations of dealing with the French bureaucracy, the missionaries maintained cordial relationships with the authorities.

As far as national, European, or world politics were concerned, the missionaries took notice only when a crisis seemed grave enough to imperil their continued residence in France. There were three occasions when they worried about the possibility of a forced evacuation: the Hungarian and Suez crises of 1956, the unrest caused by the Algerian situation in the early 1960's, and the events of May 1968. Some of the

alarmist rhetoric in newsletters may have played upon
the fears of American readers, but there was enough
concern expressed in sketchily drawn evacuation plans
and in business correspondence with mission headquarters to indicate genuine fears that political
events might terminate the American missionary presence in France.[49] Evangelicals recalled the fate
of Christian missions in postwar China, and they frequently warned about what could happen in a country
with an active communist party. This fostered the
only clearly expressed political theme of their work:
anti-communism.

Most of the missionaries' anti-communist statements came in their newsletters and mission magazine
articles, indicating that it was a concern which they
shared more with their supporting constituency than
with mission leaders in the home office. When they
wrote about communism in official correspondence it
was usually in a dispassionate description of the
political sentiments of a local neighborhood or even
of individuals in whom the missionaries were interested. However, the reports designed for public consumption were more likely to emphasize the national
strength of communism or even international conspira-
torial schemes. Most of the anti-communist material
written by the missionaries circulated in the early
and mid-1950's. Although by this time most political
observers saw that the influence of communism in
France had ebbed to a stable level, in America anti-
communist sentiment prevailed. The warnings and
appeals were high-pitched. One account of missionary
life in France described a visit to a communist
rally:

> The initial chill I had felt creeping up my
> spine soon wore into the tingling excitement
> of conspiracy. We were spies on enemy
> territory. After the rally my knees were not
> too steady as we threaded our way out amid
> the cheering comrades. Vitality had been
> drained through this head-on encounter with
> the enemy.[50]

The most strident appeals stressed the urgency of the
situation:

> The only hope for Europe in this critical
> hour is Christianity! If we do not reach
> these benighted people before communism does

156

they are doomed! What has happened in China, in Tibet, in inner Mongolia, in North Korea, and now in Indo-China in the Orient is happening before our very eyes in country after country in Europe today.[51]

But if the missionaries were alarmed about communism, they suggested no course of political action, and offered no solution to the problem except for the conversion of Frenchmen to Biblical Christianity. They were less concerned about the political power of communism than by its atheistic aspect. Again, their doctrinal stance shaped their attitude toward an aspect of French society and culture. Communism's main offense was that it blinded many Frenchmen to true religion. In fact, the missionaries distinguished little difference between communism and Catholicism. The philosophical and political enmity between French Catholicism and communism made little impact upon the missionary attitude. In official reports, articles, and newsletters communism and Catholicism were mentioned in the same breath as joint enemies of the gospel in France. The missionaries labeled them both as false religions.[52]

The problems French culture posed for the evangelicals persisted throughout the postwar period. Missionaries traditionally went to societies whose beliefs and customs were incompatible with the precepts of Christianity. But these societies were usually ignorant of Christianity, and while the missionaries sought to achieve enough cultural empathy and identification to earn the right to be heard, they offered something new and different. In most mission fields the invitation to embrace a new religion brought with it modern medical care, new school facilities, and agricultural assistance. Although mission executives stressed that these costly and time-consuming activities remained subordinate to the primary mission goal of evangelization, these ancillary benefits nonetheless encouraged belief in a religion which seemed true and, in a linear view of history, progressive. Modern, secularized, de-Christianized France did not yield to this enticement or logic. Missionary identification with a secularized culture tended to undermine their message. Most of French society and culture, rather than merely being ignorant of Christianity, had known it, rejected it, and moved on. Where did the evangelical missionaries propose to lead the French? Backward into a past Chrstian era?

157

Forward to yet another Christian era? There was no certain trumpet. There was no clear proclamation.

The American missionaries, conforming their attitudes and behavior to the tightly held doctrines of American evangelical Christianity, found little common ground between their faith and the culture to which they had come. They were discouraged to conclude that French history and Christian history seemed to be going in different directions. A perceptive missionary call to action culminated in a passive conclusion:

> I think that our difficulty is deeper than most of us are willing to admit. It is the tremendous gulf that separates us from the people we are trying to reach.
>
> The gulf is cultural. Evangelical Christianity in France, even among our French brethren, is essentially Anglo-Saxon in its expression. The gulf is intellectual. Most of us find ourselves intellectually inferior to the people we are trying to reach, and to compensate, we reach a class of people who have little influence on others. It is philosophical. We live in a world of absolutes and they do not. And we have found a way to speak to them meaningfully only if they accept our absolutes. It is linguistic. We speak French poorly, and often fail to realize that the Frenchman hears our words in a different frame of reference than ours. The gulf is social. We have few real social contacts with the French. We are tense in unfamiliar situations. The gulf is religious. We often communicate the external trappings of our particular brand of Christianity, rather than the inner beauty . . ..
>
> Perhaps the success we see in our work is not because we are necessarily bridging the gulf, but because some French people are willing to leap over to our side in order to have Christ.[53]

[1]H. Cleveland, G. Mangone, J. Adams, The Overseas Americans (New York: Arno Press, 1980), p. 27.

[2]Cleveland, p. 28; Louis Luzbetak, The Church and Cultures (Pasadena: William Carey Library, 1976), p. 97-100.

[3]American missionaries sent to other countries almost never took language study before departure. Most judged their proficiency to be only fair. (Moyer, p. 35.)

[4]1968 Annual Conference Report, TEAM, p. 40.

[5]Chairman's Report, 1955 Annual Report, TEAM.

[6]Frank Horton, "The Right Kind of Men," His (magazine of Intervarsity Christian Fellowship), January, 1968, p. 12.

[7]Annual Reports, Social Committee Report, 1968, 1972, 1973, TEAM.

[8]1969 Annual Conference Report, TEAM, p. 23; Trifon Kalioudjoglu, undated newsletter, Christian Missions in Many Lands.

[9]Annual Report, Medical Committee Report, 1972, TEAM.

[10]McCreary, p. 233.

[11]McGavran, Understanding Church Growth (Grand Rapids: William B. Eerdmans Co., 1973), p. 198.

[12]Frank Horton, "What the French Think of Our Missionaries," Eternity, August, 1958, p. 23.

[13]World Council of Churches, p. 2.

[14]Jacques Ellul, report to Foreign Workers Conference, September, 1972.

[15]Evans, Let Europe Hear, pp. 172-173.

[16]Evans, <u>Let Europe Hear</u>, pp. 130-131; "Evangelism in France," p. 26, World Council of Churches, pp. 26, 31.

[17]James Burroughs, newsletter, November, 1963, Conservative Baptist Foreign Mission Society.

[18]For a comparative view of the problems confronting the church or a religious group in a traditional European familist/individualist society see Banfield, pp. 85-89.

[19]Mehl, p. 275; J. Blocher, "Basic . . . ," p. 1; Darwin Neddo, newsletter, February, 1970, Greater Europe Mission; S. Benetreau, "Obstacles to Evangelism," report given to meeting of AEEI, February 11, 1967.

[20]Luzbetak, pp. 111, 118,120, 141-143, 295-296.

[21]Seguy, pp. 80-81, 92-95, 117, 162, 174; Mehl, <u>Traite</u> . . ., p. 209.

[22]Cleveland, pp. 92-96.

[23]Vajko, pp. 215-216; Hedlund, pp. 161-164.

[24]Mehl, pp. 223-225, 251-254.

[25]The quotation, representative of many, is from an article by TEAM general director David Johnson, <u>Missionary Broadcaster</u>, February, 1954, TEAM, p. 2.

[26]<u>Lifeline</u>, second quarter, 1962, UFM.

[27]Evans, <u>Let Europe Hear</u>, pp. 47-59.

[28]<u>Missionary Broadcaster</u>, April, 1959, TEAM, p. 10.

[29]"Report on Tent Evangelism," Foreign Workers Conference, 1955.

[30]Weldon Clark, "Easter in France," <u>Missionary Broadcaster</u>, March 1959, TEAM, p. 9; "The Effect of Roman Catholicism on Protestant Missions in France," n.d., UFM.

[31]Frances Johnston, "French Youth Today," Power Life, March 9, 1969.

[32]Letter, Ivan Peterson to Vernon Mortenson, November 10, 1969, TEAM.

[33]Letter, Arthur Johnson to Vernon Mortenson, August 8, 1969, TEAM.

[34]"Paper on Strategy," CBFMS, n.d. (1970?).

[35]Jacques Blocher, "Basic Aspects of Effective Evangelization of France in Our Generation," notes of lecture given at meeting of the AEEI, February 11, 1962, p. 1; Henri Blocher, "Theological Orientation of Evangelism," notes of lecture given at meeting of the AEEI, February 11, 1962.

[36]Gospel Message, summer, 1976; GMU; letter, Arthur Johnston to Vernon Mortenson, August 19, 1969; letter, Ivan Peterson to Vernon Mortenson, November 10, 1969, TEAM; "Committee on Roman Catholicism Report," 1970; TEAM. For a similar dilemma in Italy, see Hedlund, pp. 232-233.

[37]See Hilkka Malaska, The Challenge for Evangelical Missions to Europe: A Scandinavian Case Study, (South Passadena: William Carey Library, 1970). This study provides corroborative insight into the presence of American missionaries in a European culture.

[38]Letter, Arthur Johnston to David Johnson, June 2, 1973, TEAM; Evans, Let Europe Hear, p. 100.

[39]Blocher, Influence, p. 21; interview with Blocher, June 15, 1973.

[40]Letters, Arthur Johnston to Vernon Mortenson, December 5, 1972, March 10, 1964, TEAM.

[41]1959 Annual Conference Report, p. 9; 1961 Annual Conference Report, p. 9; 1965 Annual Conference Report, p. 32, TEAM.

[42]Letter, Arthur Johnston to David Johnson, December 19, 1958, TEAM, is but one of many letters assuring the American offices of the doctrinal stance of Nogent.

[43]Letter, Arthur Johnston to David Johnson, September 17, 1958, TEAM.

[44]Letters, Arthur Johnston to Vernon Mortenson, May 16, 1964, Arthur Johnston to Kenneth Taylor, July 3, 1964, TEAM; 1965 Annual Conference Report, TEAM. p. 24.

[45]"Orientation," 1973 Semi-Annual Conference, Vol. II, TEAM, p. 2; "Fusion, Partnership, Collaboration," paper given by Vernon Mortenson, 1973 Semi-Annual Conference, TEAM.

[46]Letter, Jacques Dubois, pastor, Tabernacle Church, to Arthur Johnston, May 23, 1966, TEAM; Blocher, Influence . . ., pp. 12-13.

[47]Stotts, pp. vi, 305; Chery, pp. 320, 321; Kane, p. 548; Marcel Tabailloux, ed., Annuaire Evangélique, 1965, 1966, 1968, (Grenoble: Defi); Frederick Fogel, "Current Methods of Evangelism Used by Pentecostals in French-Speaking Europe," lecture given to Foreign Workers Conference, 1964; Stephan, p. 258.

[48]Fogel, Ibid; Kalioudjoglou, newsletter, n.d. Christian Missions in Many Lands.

[49]John Jesberg, newsletter, November, 1956, TEAM; Frances Johnston, Rendezvous with Paris (Chicago: Moody Press, 1964), p. 52; 1965 Annual Report, Minutes of Board of Trustees meeting, June 27, 1968, Greater Europe Mission.

[50]Frances Johnston, Rendezvous with Paris, pp. 80-83.

[51]J. Jesberg, newsletter, 1952, TEAM.

[52]D. Johnson, Missionary Broadcaster, February, 1954, TEAM, p. 2; Evans, Let Europe Hear, p. 109.

[53]Thomas Julien, "Church Growth and Total Strategy," Foreign Workers Conference, 1969.

CHAPTER VII

CONCLUSION

By 1975 the American evangelical missionary enterprise in France was firmly established. The failure of itinerant evangelism in the immediate post-war years had convinced American mission leaders that the evangelization of France could be accomplished only by a resident missionary force. The most persistent trend in the story of American evangelical missions in France was the steady rise in the number of missionaries. The handful of missionaries who went to France in the late 1940's grew to over fifty by 1952, and to over one hundred by 1957. The 1960's saw an even greater increase, especially at the end of the decade. In 1965 there were over 175 American evangelical missionaries in France, and in 1970 over 250. By 1975 the figure approached 375 (representing nearly 40 mission agencies), with plans for continued expansion at an accelerated rate.

The missionaries concentrated their efforts on major urban centers in France: Bordeaux, Grenoble, Marseille, and Paris. Over one-half of the total missionary population worked in the Paris suburbs, but only half a dozen in Paris itself. The rest of the missionaries were scattered unevenly. Thirty-eight departments in France revealed no missionary presence, and an additional twelve included but one missionary couple. The missionaries did not find measurably greater receptivity to their work in any particular region of France.

The missionaries counted the establishment of a large Bible school and over fifty churches as their most visible and most significant achievements. The European Bible Institute was founded in the early years of the postwar missionary work, but it was not until after a decade or more of unsuccessful work in a variety of faltering projects that most missions adopted the strategy of establishing new churches. The most productive years for the missionaries were the late 1960's and early 1970's, when they saw a sharp increase not only in the number of missionaries, but also in the number of new churches and in the size of the French community with which the missionaries worked. For example, the total weekly attendance at the churches established by the Evangelical Alliance

Mission rose from fifty in 1959 to 270 in 1965, to 375 in 1970, and then 650 in 1975.[1]

It is difficult to evaluate the activity on which the missionaries placed the highest priority: the conversion of Frenchmen to evangelical Christianity. Few kept accurate records of conversions. Most missionaries engaged in evangelism thought that they averaged ten or fifteen a year. However conversion tally sheets could be misleading. Some of those converted never joined an evangelical church, and others, perhaps as many as 50%, eventually lost interest entirely. Although the missionaries did not keep accurate numerical records of their evangelistic success and failure, they maintained that the evangelization of France remained their ultimate goal. Accordingly, they directed their energies to evangelism and establishing churches, and did not involve themselves in organized social work. The highly-regarded Mennonite workshop for the retarded was a notable exception. Some of the missionaries worked to ameliorate social problems on an individual basis by aiding French families suffering from poverty, alcoholism, or disturbed children.

The missionaries' evaluation of their efforts in evangelization and establishing churches revealed different standards and perceptions. The Americans attached to large missions with several growing churches evaluated their work statistically, while those involved in small groups tended to ignore numbers and stress qualitative factors. While the missionary force included a few personalities who refused to confess any failure (everything they did became a valuable experience), most of the American evangelical missionaries admitted that the results of their evangelistic efforts were slim.

The American evangelical missionaries made their greatest impact in France within the French evangelical community. The establishment of nearly fifty new churches by the Americans counted as a major achievement when compared to the inability of the French evangelicals to increase significantly the number and size of their congregations. Although some of the new churches were very small, other boasted congregations and buildings large enough to give the evangelicals greater visibility and identity in their local communities.

The contribution of the Americans to French evangelical education was equally important. The European Bible Institute grew to full stature, and became a focal point for many evangelical activities in France. By 1970 three of the four evangelical institutions serving French-speaking Europe (the European Bible Institute, Vaux-sur-Seine, Nogent, and Emmaus) were headed by Americans. It was within the context of education that the Americans exerted influence upon the theology of French evangelicals. The missionaries' emphasis upon the inspiration of Scripture, the theology of evangelism, and the doctrine of premillennialism made inroads into French evangelical thought.

In addition to making institutional and theological contributions, the Americans influenced the programs and activity of the French evangelicals. Most important, as both the French and the Americans freely acknowledged, the French evangelicals became more aggressive evangelists. American-led evangelistic campaigns brought to the French evangelicals not only a new sense of priorities, but also a new sense of unity. As the French became more involved in evangelism they overcame initial reluctance to use American methods, and later readily utilized techniques like dial-a-prayer, widespread literature distribution, and use of mass media. The missionaries revitalized some French congregations by encouraging Sunday school development and increased lay involvement in church worship and service. The American missionaries broadened the horizons of the French evangelicals, and sent several French evangelical leaders to the United States on speaking tours or for additional training.

The financial aspect of the missionary activity formed a large part of the American contribution to the French evangelicals. Sometimes the Americans provided direct financial assistance in the form of grants or loans. But usually the financial contribution was indirect, in the form of literature, equipment, buildings, and the services of the missionaries. Although it is impossible to ascertain the exact figure spent by the Americans in France, the total investment of the postwar missionary endeavor mounted to several million dollars.

The growth of American influence on the evangelical work in France was best illustrated by the changed attitude of the French evangelical leaders. The

opposition and even hostility which greeted the initial missionary activity was replaced by cooperation
and even gratitude. Although French evangelical leaders preferred American missionaries to attach their
work to an existing French church or institution, they
came to the point where they could overlook bothersome
cultural differences in order to affirm the importance
of the American missionaries' contribution to the
vitality of the evangelical community in France.

Although the missionaries were pleased with their
influence upon the French evangelicals, this was not
the purpose for which they had come to France. They
had planned to make an impact upon France itself, not
merely upon their co-religionists in that country.
But by 1975 their efforts remained unnoticed by most
Frenchmen. The meager results led to high rates of
missionary frustration and attrition. Theological
differences separated them from most Frenchmen, but so
did a large number of cultural and social barriers.
Most missionaries never overcame their linguistic
handicap, and many encountered difficulty in adapting
to French culture. The concentration of their efforts
on the lower middle class, and their reluctance or
inability to penetrate the upper and lower classes,
lessened further their influence.

The missionaries in France, both individually and
as a group, lacked clearly defined goals. Intermis-
sion planning and cooperation was minimal, leading to
apparent confusion and costly duplication of effort.
Some missions were plagued by poor management, either
in France or in the home office. Those with a rigid
authority structure often stifled individual initiative, while loosely organized missions often lacked
leadership and a clear sense of purpose. The mission
headquarters in America played a major role in the
missionary enterprises in France, and some pursued
ill-advised programs which caused friction within the
mission. Policies concerning the recruitment and preparation of missionary candidates were especially
inadquate.

Confusion in management led to confusion in
methods. The missionaries often imparted the traditions and trappings of midwestern fundamentalism with
little concern for the French religious heritage.
American evangelistic strategies pressed for immediate
"decisions for Christ", and their church membership
policies often insisted upon high standards of social

behavior. While this may have ensured commitment and propriety among converts, it did little to attract those who might be interested to learn but not ready to decide.

The small groups begun by the missionaries were often weakened by negative dynamics stemming from organizational and leadership problems. Missionary pastors overcame group lethargy by doing all the work. This may have led to some definite accomplishments, but it increased the likelihood that the group would disintegrate when the missionary withdrew. Groups with a believing but inactive laity and an active pastor were unlikely to grow.

Only rarely did the missionaries realize that much of their activity was counter-productive. Most assumed that response to their appeals and programs was either positive or indifferent (neutral). However, the normal response was either positive or negative. When the missionaries persisted in activity which drew frequent negative responses, they actually built a consensus against them, limiting even further their impact.

Even when they seized upon a method or a program which was productive, they often failed to follow it through. Sooner or later almost all the missionaries agreed that their primary task was the establishment of new churches, but they vacillated in applying this strategy. Part of the problem lay in their inability to determine what, exactly, comprised a church. Some missionaries denied the legitimacy of the Roman Catholic church and the French Reformed church, but recognized as a church a handful of newly converted French people meeting in a rented hall. Others resisted the proliferation of tiny storefront congregations by insisting upon appropriate minimal standards for church size, organization, and affiliation. Successful church organizers left that activity to follow other pursuits. Institutions like the European Bible Institute, although emphasizng support for the strategy of establishing churches, did little to train Frenchmen for that specific task. Most of its graduates became itinerant evangelists or filled positions in existing churches. Some even went to Africa instead of remaining to work in France. Very few were engaged in the establishment of new churches which all evangelicals agreed was the task of paramount importance.

Even when the missionaries devoted themselves wholeheartedly to establishing a church they confronted many dilemmas. Because conversions were relatively difficult to achieve, many of the new evangelical churches were built upon transfers. Therefore the growth of one church resulted in the decline in the numbers of an evangelical group elsewhere.

The missionaries agreed that they needed several middle-class French families to form the core of a new church. But it was more common for single people, women, the very young, the very old, and non-French to be attracted to the evangelical groups. Again, negative dynamics hindered church growth. The more the church's social image became non-French, single, or female, the less likely it became that the needed middle-class families would join.

Even after a church had been organized it faced major problems. One was the small size of the evangelical churches. All but a handful counted fewer than sixty members. Often the initial growth was relatively rapid when the missionary devoted his time to evangelism and organizing the church. But once the church was organized the missionary usually found his energy consumed by church administration and problems within the group. There was little time for evangelism and recruiting new members, and therefore growth leveled off. By 1970 most missionaries believed that it took a minimum of ten years to establish a viable church, while some contended that it took as long as twenty or twenty-five years.

Economic considerations stifled church growth. A church building and a French pastor were the two big expenses. A deep division split the missionaries on the question of church buildings. Some insisted that an attractive church structure was necessary to convince the French that evangelicals were serious, respectable, and established. A good church building, they said, would save five years of work. Other missionaries were adamantly opposed to the purchase of property and the construction of a building by a small evangelical group. Buildings, this faction of missionaries maintained, diverted energy and time from religious concerns to the technical details of construction. And a building usually saddled a small group with a large and demoralizing debt.

The economics of church buildings was closely connected to the question of supporting a French pastor. It took a long time for missionaries to come to the point where they decided to place their churches under the control of a French pastor. But even if the missionaries were willing, the congregation was often unable to raise enough money to support a pastor. A large building debt made it less likely that a congregation could afford its own pastor. After thirty years of American missionary work in France there were few churches which the missionaries had left in the hands of a French successor.

Even when all the obstacles were overcome and a church established, the issue of the church's affiliation raised new problems. Some missions welded their new churches into an association of their own design. This provided a framework in which the new churches could assist each other, but it also increased greatly their sectarian image, created a new subdivision within the already fragmented French evangelical community. This also preserved the American flavor of the churches. Other new churches were determined to remain autonomous and independent. Refusing any wider affiliation, they suffered from isolation and vague identity. Others spent a great deal of time debating the issues of affilation and cooperation without being able to decide one way or the other.

By 1975 the American evangelical missionaries in France realized reluctantly that their growing numbers and their persistent efforts had yielded small results. They wanted to make an impact upon France, but they were forced to be content with the impact they made upon the tiny evangelical miniority in France. A few felt that their only impact was upon the lives of some individual Frenchmen. Christians who were taught the immeasurable worth of a single lost sheep could take comfort in this type of achievement, but they continued to evaluate their efforts, hoping to find the reasons for their failure and a formula for greater success. There were some who said that discouragement was premature. Taking a long view, they compared the missionary experience in France with that in China where the first generation of missionary work produced little, but was followed by years of broad expansion and significant achievement. Other missionaries, while admitting that perhaps twenty-five years of missionary work in a society was not enough time to yield a conclusive judgment, maintained that France was not China, and the comparison was inappropriate.

In general there were three basic views of the problems which the missionaries faced in France. A few missionaries said that the problems could be overcome by energy, hard work, efficient organization, and effective leadership. They affirmed that the small degree of success which had already been won usually was achieved by missions which were controlled by one leader with authority and a clear sense of purpose. Other missionaries were convinced that the problems were deep and complex, and that simply trying harder would not do. They were divided between a group which decided that the problems were primarily sociological and a group which maintained that the problems were basically theological.

The two groups debated the role of the missionary in French society. Those who stressed the sociological nature of the problems said that the failure of American missions in France was largely due to cultural differences. They were disturbed by the bold American behavior of many missionaries which they said offended most Frenchmen. Missionary work in France, they insisted, could succeed only if the missionaries adapted completely to French culture and became assimilated into French society.

The other group of missionaries was discouraged by the weakness of French evangelical Christianity and by the large areas of conflict which they discerned between French culture and evangelical Christianity. They concluded that the theological or doctrinal differences separated them from Frenchmen more than did cultural differences. They stressed the theological conversion of Frenchmen rather than cultural adaptation of the missionaries.

The two groups, of course, were not mutually exclusive. Although they differed in emphasis, their activity remained similar. Those in the first group maintained their evangelical goals while attempting greater cultural adaptation. The second group made progress in conforming to French customs while stressing doctrinal issues. The missionaries who emphasized cultural issues often achieved better rapport with the French evangelicals, and they were largely responsible for the continuing progress in cultural adaptation made by all the American missionaries in France. But they overlooked the weakness of the French evangelicals, and they could not point to conclusive evidence indicating that missionary success was proportional to cultural adaptation.

The missionaries who claimed to be more concerned about doctrinal differences than cultural differences perceived the wide gap between modern French society and evangelical Christianity. The many points of opposition between French culture and evangelical doctrine persuaded them that cultural assimilation was an unlikely path to conversion. Excessive concern with cultural adaptation, they said, only skirted the issue. If cultural assimilation were the way to conversion, they maintained, the French evangelicals would have been more successful. However, they overlooked the sectarian image of the independent French evangelicals and arbitrarily limited true Christianity in France to their small camp.

But these differences of opinion among the missionaries were insignificnt in comparison to the division between them and French society. Even the most culturally adaptable missionaries held doctrinal positions which separated them from most groups in French society. They found it difficult to conform to the society which they had come to convert. Cultural adaptation was proscribed by theological conviction. The American evangelical missionaries carved out an insular position for themselves in French society.

Ironically their isolation was underscored by the most successful example of their cultural assimilation, their relationship with the independent French evangelicals. The American missionaries in France arrived with no status in French society. Therefore the French did not know how to regard them. At first, the Americans saw no need to achieve status within French culture. If they thought about the issue at all, they presumed that the identity of their American evangelical group or denomination would carry similar weight in France. A few missionaries never moved past this point. They operated in their own orbit in France puzzled that so few French people knew who they were or what they were doing. By the 1960's most missions realized that they had to achieve status in France by identifying themselves with some Christian group in French society. The missionaries never

considered identifying themselves with the largest
Christian group in France, Roman Catholicism. On the
contrary, their intense doctrinal opposition to
Catholicism compelled them to stress their distance
from Rome. A desire for a French affiliation would
not erase theological incompatibility and 450 years of
history since the Reformation. But the missionaries
also shunned the doors of the Reformed Church, even
though they counted 50,000 evangelicals within its
fold. This was the lost opportunity for the first
generation of modern American evangelical missionary
work in France.

Instead, many missionaries chose, somewhat haphazardly and incompletely, to identify themselves with
the small evangelical denominations like the Baptists,
Brethren, or Free Churches. But these French groups
wielded almost no influence in France, and commanded
little status. The American missionaries chose this
association because these evangelicals and their doctrine seemed familiar, not because they offered a
strategic advantage to the mission work in France. A
few other missions took an even narrower path, kept to
themselves, associated with no French group, and projected a funamentalist and separatist image.

One alternative to identifying the missionary
work with small little-known evangelical denominations
or associations was to avoid purposefully any identity
with ecclesiastical institutions. This approach presumed that the de-Christianized areas of France or
segments of French society would not respond to overtures from the institutional church, but would confront Christianity on neutral ground. The Grace
Brethren chateau at Saint-Albain embodied this concept, but this innovative and useful evangelistic
tactic needed to refer the people it attracted to
established Christian churches and institutions. The
missionaries at the chateau envisioned it as a bridge
between a de-Christianized society and Christianity,
and they did not intend converts to remain on the
bridge. The entire American missionary force could
not assume a neutral stance between the secular and
the religious. The neutral bridge concept could function only if there were a Christian community on the
other side. The missionaries and the French evangelicals formed part of that community, but their sectarian image made them uninviting.

A more challenging approach, an opportunity rarely pondered and never attempted, advocated missionary cooperation with the most prominent Protestant denomination in France, the Reformed church. Although not without great problems, this course of action would have gone a long way to solve the missionaries' painful lack of status and identity in French society. A cordial relationship with the Reformed church had much to offer the missionaries in France. Although small compared to the Roman Catholic church in France, the Reformed church enjoyed a historic prestige and a reputation for integrity and patriotism. Identification with this respected French institution offered a way to dispel the alien image of the missionaries, helping them to avoid the stigma attached to the Mormons, Jehovah's Witnesses, and other foreign sects. The evangelical contention that the Reformed church had lapsed into lethargy, unconcerned about evangelization, was on the mark. But a minority within the Reformed church took seriously the imperative of regathering all the unattached Protestants in the newly mobile population of modern France. The Reformed church's home mission organization, the Societe Centrale de'Evangélisation, attracted French Protestants who took seriously their evangelistic duty. The Protestant communities at Taizé and Chambon-sur-Lignon presented an attractive image of Protestantism, especially to French youth. A movement attached to the Reformed church was more likely to engender the social and religious change the missionaries sought in France than one wearing an evangelical or American label. Evangelization in connection with the Reformed church invited converts to join an established and venerable French form of Christianity rather than an isolated foreign sect.

But this idea unsettled the American missionaries. Raising their profile in France did not seem worth the risks they saw in being associated with a liberal denomination. They guarded their clear doctrinal stance and their autonomy. Missions insisted on maintaining control over their own destiny in France, no matter how small their impact. Their primary goal had become not the widespread proclamation of the gospel and Christian ethics, but control of their own converts and churches. They wanted to protect them from liberal or pentecostal ideas which ran counter to standard evangelical doctrine. Accountability to the home office and to the missionaries' American supporters weighed heavily. These people were not likely to countenance activity in France unlike that at home. So the missionaries established churches and church associations (like TEAM's AEEI) with strict policies designed to ensure the long-term fidelity of their achievements in France.

Some missionaries offered historical justification for this stance. This was yet another way in which Robert Evans shaped the American missionary movement in France. In the early 1970's, more than twenty years after he had led the way for postwar missions in France and had founded the European Bible Institute, Evans earned his Ph.D. from the University of Manchester. In his dissertation on the role of foreign missionaries in the nineteenth century Protestant Réveil, Evans concluded that almost all of the new churches established during the Réveil had been taken over by the Reformed church later in the century because they lacked clear, strict, and distinguishing church policies. Accordingly, he cautioned the missionaries to maintain a vigilant watch over church policies and affiliations if they wished to avoid eventually being swallowed up by the liberal Reformed church. This note struck a responsive chord in most of the missionaries who came from small evangelical denominations in America which had seceded from larger denominations in protest over their drift toward liberal theology.

There was a certain irony in the zeal for orthodox institutions. In the foregoing two or three generations, American evangelicals had seen one institution after another (churches, colleges, seminaries) abandon conservative theology in favor of more liberal ideas. The evangelicals responded to institutional failure by founding their own institutions, which in time fell prey to similar infidelity. Perhaps this testified to little more than the impermanence of human institutions. But Evans' admonition encouraged those who wished to preserve the missionary institutions as long as possible.

What little possibility there was that American evangelicals would make overtures to the Reformed church (and vise versa) was swept aside completely when the church growth movement captured mission planners in the 1960's. This did not follow logically. Church growth advocates looked to New Testament models for instruction in evangelization and church growth. The apostolic method sought interested people at the places of religion. In the first Christian century that was the synagogue, the place of prayer, or even Mars Hill. In twentieth century France it was the churches, Catholic and Reformed. But the missionaries were hamstrung by American evangelical aversion to Catholicism and liberal Protestantism, so they avoided the places where people interested in Christianity were most likely to be found. Furthermore, the church growth movement's global strategy implied that missionaries to secular France might best serve in association with existing churches. The church growth movement mandated the effective multiplication of churches in the world's receptive societies. Mission resources were to be allocated accordingly. France was obviously an unreceptive society, so the theory suggested it should have attracted a comparatively small missionary investment, perhaps a holding action in cooperation with the churches planted centuries before. New churches established under a loose affiliation with the Reformed church could have assumed the form of semi-autonomous satellite congregations rather than separatist competitors. The Reformed church's several empty sanctuaries could have obviated the economic crunch when missionary churches needed a building.

Some American missionaries worked with French Reformed churches in the postwar era. But these were usually non-evangelical "fraternal workers" commissioned to France by the American mainline denominations whose theology the evangelicals found wanting. Fraternal workers subordinated their work to a French pastor, and did not seek to change French religious belief. They enjoyed identity with the French, but did not desire to change the status quo. The evangelicals desired to change the status quo, but lacked the necessary identity.

Some missions rejected completely the concept of fraternal workers because it undermined firm American control of the missionaries and their work. They opposed the idea of affiliation, no matter how compatible the French partner. However, in the 1960's a growing number of evangelical missions warmed to the idea of fraternal workers, but insisted upon complete doctrinal agreement with French partners. The Gospel Missionary Union's bond with the Free Chruch, the Alpine Mission's collaboration with French Brethren assemblies, the Mennonite alliance with French Mennonites, and the Southern Baptist projects carried

175

on with the Baptist Federation were the smoothest and
most well-accepted missionary ventures in France.
With the right personalities and considerable tact on
both sides, fraternal worker relationships with French
evangelical denominations prospered and brought
greater success to both the French and Americans. The
missionaries appeared to be strengthening the French
churches rather than competing with them. National
differences lessened. These missionaries raised no
objection to subordinating Americans to Frenchmen, but
they did oppose subordinating evangelicals to
nonevangelicals. They claimed to fear confusion among
the French people they contacted as well as among
their supporters at home if they were identified with
a liberal church or denomination. Financial
implications forbade this type of initiative. American evangelicals were unlikely to continue financial
support to any mission associated with liberal denominations, or the ecumenical movement. Proponents of
an evangelical connection with the Reformed church in
France urged individual missionaries to by-pass this
roadblock by seeking denominational mission support
from an American denomination like the Presbyterians
who maintained connections with the Reformed Church in
France. But this option could have supported only a
few. Evangelical missions depended on American individuals and churches for financial support, and could
not afford to offend them with controversial ventures.
The home front directed the strategy.

Pursuing a relationship between the evangelical
missionaries and the French Reformed church would have
required a significant shift in American mission
theory and practice. It also would have required a
large amount of courage and faith. In some instances,
on an individual level, the problems would have been
minimal. There were a few conservative pastors and
many parishioners (perhaps half the total evangelical
population of France) in the Reformed church who
shared the missionaries' evangelical doctrines. A
partnership along these lines would have strengthened
the Reformed evangelicals and encouraged them to
gather in the dispersed inactive Protestants or to use
their position in the respected Reformed church to
evangelize the French population.

Larger problems loomed between an evangelical
missionary and liberal Reformed pastor. There would
have been squabbles (all the missionaries engaged in
these with French associates from time to time) and

even sharp disagreements. But if a Reformed pastor had agreed to cooperate with an American missionary, their doctrinal differences probably would have been more of a problem for the missionary (and his supporters) than to the Frenchman. Collaboration, even if marked by differences, could have profited both. American missionaries linked to the Reformed church would have achieved access to parts of French society and earned an audience otherwise denied them, while the overworked Protestant pastors would have acquired helping hands for mounting pastoral duties. The activity of the missionaries would have been focused upon increasing the personal spiritual strength of parishioners and congregations rather than ensuring the longevity of institutions. If historical precedent indicated the eventual absorption of missionary contributions by the Reformed church, some critics counselled the American missionaries to focus their contributions on that institution from the beginning. But American missions were unwilling to sacrifice control for the sake of an expanded personal impact of the missionaries. The faith missions, as they called themselves, had more faith that their financial needs would be met than that their converts would be sustained without a tightly controlled religious environment.

So, the American evangelical missionaries eschewed relationships or identification with the major Christian denominations in France. Holding out a hand once in a while to minor evangelical groups, they continued to plod along, usually concentrating on their individual projects. Forming a small part of the postwar American involvement in Europe and a small part of the postwar expansion of evangelical missions, they were among the least successful of each. But few could match their dedication and resiliant confidence. They saw their task as history's highest calling and challenge. They suffered continual disappointment, but worked diligently and compassionately among people who usually considered them anomalous or anachronistic, if they bothered to pay them any attention at all. Their discouragement in French society did not convince them that their endeavor was futile. Instead, they increased their numbers and their effort. The evangelical beliefs which limited their acceptance by the French also sustained their persistence. They were content to work against the grain of European history in the twentieth century. While the French converted empty churches into garages, the

American missionaries converted garages into churches.

CHAPTER VII NOTES

[1]Vajko, p. 252.

SOURCES

Although published sources for this study remain scanty, mission agency archives help to fill the gap. However, the widely dispersed agencies differed in the diligence with which they maintained records. A few missions kept almost no records whatsoever, while others accumulated every scrap of paper which dealt with their work in France. The main problem encountered in using these materials was disorder. Some missions adhered to alphabetical or chronological order in their filing systems, but most preferred novel systems of their own design. Inaccessibility sometimes frustrated the study when a few mission boards refused to open their files. However, most were candid and cooperative, providing annual reports, minutes of business meetings, official and sometimes private correspondence, position papers, newsletters, brochures, and articles. Discontinuity proved more of a problem than inaccessibility. Annual reports, for instance, might be missing because they had been misplaced, or sometimes because they never had been written. Fortunately the largest and most important missions were the ones which possessed the most accurate records as well as the greatest willingness to make them available. Furthermore, historical scholarship concerned with the recent past, when thwarted by sensitivity about the release of written documents, compensates by conversation with the participants. Many of the individuals mentioned in this study supplied valuable and corroborative information, although self-serving comments needed to be filtered. Four avenues brought information from the missionaries: (1) personal correspondence; (2) personal interviews, (3) taped response by a missionary to questions sent by the author; (4) written questionnaires, completed by the missionaries. More than 230 missionaries responded through at least one of these forms of communication, and usually through three or four. Similar approaches supplied information from mission executives in the American offices and from Frenchmen who were informed about American missionary work in their country.

BIBLIOGRAPHY

Books

Allen, R.: Missionary Methods: St. Paul's or Our's?. Grand Rapids: William B. Eerdmans Publishing Co., 1962.

Ardagh, J.: The New French Revolution. New York: Harper, Row Publishers, 1968.

Bailey, H. and Jackson, H.: A Study of Missionary Motivation, Training, and Withdrawal. New York: Missionary Research Library, 1965.

Banfield, E.: The Moral Basis of a Backward Society. Chicago: The Free Press (University of Chicago), 1958.

Beaujeu-Garnier, J.: La Population Francaise. Paris, Librarie Armand Colin, 1969.

Benoit, J.: Denominations et sectes en France. Paris: Librarie Protestante, 1965.

Bible Christian Union.: The Story of the Bible Christian Union. New York: Bible Christian Union, n.d.

Bishop, C.: France Alive. New York: McMullen Company, 1947.

Boegner, M. and Siegfried, A.: Protestantisme Francais. Paris: Librairie Plan, 1945.

Bost, C.: Histoire des Protestantes de France, 4th ed. Paris: La Carese, 1957.

Boulard, F.: An Introduction to Religious Society. London: Dalton, Longman, and Todd, 1960.

Budd, S.: Sociologists and Religion. London: Collier-Macmillan Publishers, 1973.

Butterfield, H.: Christianity in European History. London: Collins, 1952.

182

Carrier, H. and Pin, E.: Essais de Sociologie Religieuse. Paris: P.U.F., 1956.

Chadwick, C.: The Secularization of the European Mind in the Nineteenth Century. Cambridge: Cambridge University Press, 1975.

Charlton, D.: Secular Religions in France: 1815-1870. London: Oxford University Press, 1963.

Chéry, H.: L'Offensive des Sectes. Paris: Les Editions du Cerf, 1959.

Cleveland, H., Mangone, G., and Adams, J.: The Overseas Americans. New York: Arno Press, 1980.

Colinion, M.: Le Phénomene des Sectes au XXe Siècle. Paris: Librairie Arthème Fayard, 1959.

Conord, P.: Protestantisme Francais d'aujourd'hui. Paris: A. Coueslant, 1959.

Coutrot, A. and Dreyfus, F.: Les Forces Religieuses dans la Societé Francaise. Paris: Librairie Armand Colin, 1965.

Coxhill, H.W., and Grubb, K. (eds.): World Christian Handbook. New York: Abingdon Press, 1968.

Dagon, G. (ed.): Petites Eglises de France. Saverne: Imprimerie Savernoise, 1966-73.

Dansette, A.: Religious History of Modern France. New York: Herder and Herder Co., 1961.

Dawson, C.: Progress and Religion. Garden City, N.Y.: Image Books, 1960.

Ellul, J.: The New Demons, tr. C. Hopkins. New York: Seabury Press, 1975.

Evans, R.: Let Europe Hear. Chicago: Moody Press, 1963.

.: Transformed Europeans. Chicago: Moody Press, 1963.

Fédération Protestante de France.: La France Protestant, Valence: Imprimeries Réunies, 1956, 1967, 1974.

Glover, R.: The Progress of World Wide Missions. New
York: Harper Brothers, 1960.

Goddard, B. (ed.): Encyclopedia of Modern Christian
Missions. Camden, N.J.: Thomas Nelson and Sons,
1967.

Godin, H.: La France: Pays de Mission. Paris: Ed.
Abeille, 1943.

Gramont, S.: The French. New York: G. P. Putnam and
Sons, 1969.

Groethuysen, B.: Origines de l'Espirit en France
(L'Eglise et la Bourgeoisie). Paris: Librairie
Gallimard, 1927.

Groethuysen, B.: "Secularism," Encyclopedia of Social
Sciences. New York: MacMillan, 1948.

Guittée, F.: Histoire de l'Eglise de France. Paris:
Bureau de l'administration de l'histoire de l'Eglise
de France, 1856.

Hallie, P.: Lest Innocent Blood Be Shed. New York:
Harper, 1979.

Harris, W. S.: Eyes on Europe. London: Hodder and
Stoughton Co., 1965.

Hayles, E.: The Catholic Church in the Modern World.
Garden City, N.Y.: Hanover House, 1958.

Hedlund, R.: The Protestant Movement in Italy. South
Pasadena: Willilam Carey Library, 1970.

Hefley, J.: God Goes to High School. Waco, Texas:
Word Books, 1970.

Hershberger, G.: The Mennonite Church in the Second
World War. Scottsdale, Pa.: Mennonite Publishing
Co., 1951.

Houghton, L.: Handbook of French and Belgian Protestantism. New York: Federal Council of the Churches
of Christ in America, 1919.

International Congress on World Evangelization.: Status of Christianity Country Profile France. Lausanne, 1974.

Johnson, D. (ed.): A Brief History of the International Fellowship of Evangelical Students. Lausanne: International Fellowship of Students, 1964.

Johnston, F.: Rendezvous With Paris. Chicago: Moody Press, 1964.

Kane, J.: A Global View of Christian Missions. Grand Rapids: Baker Book House, 1971.

        .: The Making of a Missionary. Grand Rapids: Baker Book House, 1975.

        .: Winds of Change in the Christian Mission. Chicago: Moody Press, 1973.

Kellar, A.: Christian Europe Today. New York: Harper Brothers, 1942.

Latourette, K.S.: The Christian World Mission in Our Day. New York: Harper Brothers, 1954.

        .: Christianity in a Revolutionary Age. Vol. II: The Nineteenth Century in Europe. Vol. IV: The Twentieth Century in Europe. New York: Harper Brothers, 1959, 1961.

        .: A History of the Expansion of Christianity. Vol. I: The First Five Centuries. Vol. IV: The Great Century: Europe and the United States. Vol. VII: Advance Through Storm. Grand Rapids: Zondervan Publishing House, 1970.

        .: Missions and the American Mind. Indianapolis: National Foundation Press, 1949.

LeBras, G.: Etudes de Sociologie Religieuse. Paris: Universitaires de France, 1955.

Leonard, E.: Histoire Générale du Protestantisme. Vol. III: Declin et Renouveau. Paris: Presses Universitaires de France, 1964.

        .: Le Protestante Francaise. Paris: Presses Universitaires de France, 1953.

<u>Life World Library</u>: France. New York: Time, Inc., 1961.

Lindsell, H.: <u>A Christian Philosophy of Missions</u>. Wheaton: Van Kampen Press, 1949.

Luzbetak, L.: <u>The Church and Cultures</u>. South Pasadena: William Carey Library, 1976.

Malaska, H.: <u>The Challenge for Evangelical Missions to Europe: A Scandanavian Case Study</u>. South Pasadena: William Carey Library, 1970.

Mandrou, R.: <u>Histoire des Protestants en France</u>. Toulouse: E. Privat, 1977.

Martin, D.: <u>A General Theory of Secularization</u>. New York: Harper and Row, Publishers, 1978.

Marty, M.: <u>The Modern Schism</u>. New York: Harper and Row, Publishers, 1962.

.: <u>The New Shape of American Religion</u>. New York: Harper and Brothers, 1958.

.: <u>The Public Church</u>. New York: The Crossroad Publishing Company, 1981.

.: <u>Varieties of Unbelief</u>. New York: Holt, Rinehart, and Winston, 1964.

McCreary, E.: <u>The Americanization of Europe</u>. New York: Doubleday, 1964.

McGavran, D.: <u>The Bridges of God</u>. London: World Dominion Press, 1955.

.: (ed.) <u>The Eye of the Storm</u>. Waco: World Books, 1972.

.: <u>How Churches Grow</u>. London: World Dominion Press, 1959.

.: <u>Understanding Church Growth</u>. Grand Rapids: William B. Eerdmans Publishing Co., 1970.

McLean, A.: <u>The History of the Foreign Christian Missionary Society</u>. New York: Fleming Revell, 1919.

McLoughlin, W. and Bellah, R. (eds.): Religion in America. Boston: Beacon Press, 1968.

McManners, J.: Church and State in France, 1870-1914. London: SPCK, 1972.

McQuilkin, J.: Measuring the Church Growth Movement. Chicago: Moody Press, 1973.

Mehl, R.: The Sociology of Protestantism. Philadelphia: Westminster Press, 1970.

.: Traite de Sociologie du Protestantisme. Neuchatel: Delachaux Niestle. 1965.

The Mennonite Encyclopedia. Vol. III. Scottsdale, PA.: Mennonite Publishing Company, 1956.

Merkh, D.: Europe. undated pamphlet. National Association of Free Will Baptists.

Missionary Research Library.: Directory of North American Protestant Foreign Missionary Agencies. New York: Missionary Research Library, 3rd. ed., 1958; 5th ed., 1962; 6th ed., 1964.

Missions Advanced Research and Communication Center (MARC): North American Protestant Ministries Overseas. Monrovia, CA: 9th ed., 1970; 10th ed., 1973; 12th ed., 1979.

Moberg, D.: The Church As a Social Institution. Englewood Cliffs, NJ: Prentice-Hall, 1962.

Mours, S.: Un Siècle d'évangélisation en France (1815-1914). Tome 1er, 1815-1870. Flavon, Belgium: Editions de la Librairie des Eclaireurs Unionistes, 1963.

Moyer, K.: A Study of Missionary Motivation, Training, and Withdrawal (1932-1952). New York: Missionary Research Library, 1957.

Neill, S.: A History of Christian Missions. Harmondsworth, Middlesex: Penguin, 1964.

Olmstead, C.: History of Religion in the United States. Englewood Cliffs: Prentice Hall Co., 1960.

Operation Mobilization: A Short Account of Its Beginnings, Development, and Aims. Bolton, Lancashire: Operation Mobilization, n.d.

Orna-Ornstein, F.: France: Forgotten Mission Field. London: Burlington Press. n.d. (1971?).

Pétonnet, C.: Ces Gens-là. Paris: Maspero, 1968.

Petrie, J.: The Worker Priests: A Collective Documentation. London: Routledge and Kegan Paul, 1956.

Phelps, H.: God's Deliverance From Nazi Hands. New York: European Christian Mission, 1943.

Phillips, C.: The Church in France. New York: Russell and Russell, 1966.

Robert D.: Les Eglises Réformées en France (1800-1830). Paris: Presses Universitaires de France, 1961.

Saillens, R.: The Soul of France. London: Morgan and Scott, Ltd., 1927.

Salisbury, W.: Religion in American Culture. Homewood, IL: The Dorsey Press, 1964.

Schram, S.: Protestantism and Politics in France. Alencon: Corbiere and Jugain, 1954.

Seguy, J.: Les Sectes Protestantes dans la France Contemporaine. Paris: Beauchesne et ses Fils, 1956.

Sheetz, P.: The Sovereign Hand. Wheaton: The Evangelical Alliance Mission, 1971.

Stalley, J.: No Frontiers. London, Burlington Press, n.d.

Stephan, R.: Histoire du Protestantisme Francaise. Paris: Librairie Artheme Fayard, 1961.

Steward, J.: My Story. European Evangelistic Crusade, n.d.

Trueblood, E.: The Validity of the Christian Mission. New York: Harper and Row, 1972.

U. S. Department of Commerce.: Religious Bodies: 1936. Washington, D. C., 1941.

Unruh, J.: In the Name of Christ. Scottsdale: Herald Press, 1952.

Velten, G.: Mission in Industrial France. London: SCM Press, 1968.

Verwer, G.: Literature Evangelism. Kansas City: Walterick Publishers, 1963.

Vought, D.: Protestants in Modern Spain. South Pasadena: William Carey Library, 1970.

Walsh, H.: The Concordat of 1801. New York: Columbia University Press, 1933.

Ward, M.: France Pagan? The Mission of Abbé Godin. New York: Sheed and Ward, 1949.

Watt, E.: Dynamite in Europe. London: Marshall, Morgan, and Scott, Ltd., 1947.

Winter, R.: The Twenty-five Unbelievable Years. South Pasadena: William Carey Library, 1970.

World Council of Churches.: Ecumenical Studies: Evangelism in France. Geneva: Secretariat for Evangelism of the World Council of Churches, 1951.

Zaretsky, I. and Leone, M. (eds.): Religious Movements in Contemporary America. Princeton: Princeton University Press, 1974.

Journals, Articles

Annuaire. Assemblies de Dieu de France, 1973.

Annuaire Evangélique. Grenoble: Defi, 1965, 1966, 1968, 1973.

The Brethren Missionary Herald. National Fellowship of Brethren Churches, March 1953.

Christianity Today. July 20, 1963; June 20, 1965; March 13, 1972; April 28, 1972; December 21, 1979.

Church Growth Bulletin, Institute for Church Growth Vol. IX.

Decision. Billy Graham Evangelistic Association, August 1963.

Eternity. September 1955; June 1963.

European Bible Institute Newsletter. Greater Europe Mission, December 1973.

Europe's Millions. European Christian Mission, 1946-48.

"Evangelism in France," _Ecumenical Studies_. Geneva: World Council of Churches, December 1951.

Evangelical Missions Quarterly. Winter, 1963.

Evans, R.: "Europe - Mission Field Under Camouflage," _Moody Monthly_, June, 1965.

The Fields. Christian Missions in Many Lands, July 1955, October 1963, November 1968.

Foreign Mission Echoes. National Fellowship of Brethren Churches, February 1961, March 1971.

The Gospel Message. Gospel Missionary Union, Winter 1970.

Herald. National Fellowship of Brethren Churches, November 1951.

Horton, F.: "The Right Kind of Men," _His_. Intervarsity Christian Fellowship, January 1968.

Impact. Conservative Baptist Foreign Mission Society, September 1965.

International Bulletin of Missionary Research. Vol. 6, No. 3, July, 1982. Overseas Missionary Study Center, Ventnor, N.J.

Johnston, F.: "French Youth Today," _Power Life_. March 1969.

Lifeline. Unevangelized Fields Mission, 1962.

La Morte, A.: "Moral Sag in France": _Christianity Today_. June 24, 1957.

Missionary Broadcaster. The Evangelical Alliance Mission, February 1954, May 1953, May 1955, March 1957, November 1960.

Missionary Hearld. National Fellowship of Brethren Churches, 1957.

Missions. American Baptist Foreign Mission Society, September 1919.

Moody Monthly. October 1956.

New York Times. September 24, 1966; March 17, 1977.

Newsweek. July 12, 1954; May 6, 1974.

News Bulletin. European Bible Institute, 1952.

Progress. Bible Christian Union, March 1960, December 1962.

Reporter. Greater Europe Mission, April 1960, Spring 1964, March 1966, Summer 1969.

Russel-Jones, B. "Men and Methods for Reaching Europeans." _Evangelical Missions Quarterly_, Spring, 1977.

Shank, D.: "A Missionary Approach to a Dechristianized Society," _Mennonite Quarterly Review_, Vol. XXVIII.

Time. December 27, 1982.

Unpublished Sources

Chalendeau, A.: "The Baptist Movement in French-Speaking Europe." Thesis, Northern Baptist Theological Seminary, 1960.

Dale, O.: "L'Evangélisation en Belgique Pendant l'entre-deux-guerres." Thesis, Faculté Libre de Théologie Evangélique, Vaux-sur-Seine, 1972.

Evans, R.: "The Contribution of Foreigners to the French Protestant Réveil, 1815-1850." Unpublished Ph.D. dissertation, University of Manchester, 1971.

Evans, R.: Unpublished manuscript on 1963 Operation Mobilization campaign.

Hall, M.: "The History and Methods of Mission Work by the Churches of Christ in France," Master's Thesis, Harding College Graduate School of Bible and Religion, 1959.

Hoyle, R.: "A Survey of Religion in Twentieth Century France." Master's Thesis, Columbia Bible College, n.d.

Johnston, F.: Unpublished Manuscript. TEAM. n.d.

Munn, R.: "Profiles of Grace." Unpublished manuscript, 1973.

Stotts, G.: "The History of the Modern Pentecostal Movement in France." Unpublished Ph.D. dissertation, Texas Tech University, 1973.

Vajko, R.: "A History and Analysis of the Church Planting Ministry of the Evangelical Alliance Mission in France from 1952-1974." Master's Thesis, Trinity Evangelical Divinity School, 1974.

Papers in Mission Files

Adams, W.: "Church Planting with a French Pastor." Paper delivered at Foreign Workers Conference, 1972.

Assemblies of God: Assorted brochures.

Baptist International Missions.: "Answers to Questions." Undated brochure.

Baptist Mid-Missions.: Assorted newsletters.

Baptist World Mission.: "About Our Beliefs." Undated brochure.

Barnes, W.: Newsletters, April 1972, May 1972. Evangelical Baptist Mission.

Beach, K.: "Development of New Areas: Houlgate and Lyon." TEAM, 1973.

Benetreau, S.: "Obstacles to Evangelism." Paper read to Annual Meeting of the Alliance des Eglises Evangéliques Indépendants, February 11, 1967.

Bernardo, J.: Newsletter, 1954. Alpine Mission to France.

Bible Christian Union.: Assorted newsletters and reports, 1949-1973.

Blocher, H.: "Theological Orientation of Evangelism." Notes from talk given to AEEI, February 11, 1967.

Blocher, J.: "Basic Aspects of Effective Evangelization of France in Our Generation." Notes from talk given to AEEI, February 11, 1967.

Blocher, J.: "Influence of Foreign Missionaries in France." Paper presented to TEAM semi-annual conference, November 1960.

Bonnelle, A.: Newsletters, September 1956, April 1957, April 1958. Worldwide European Fellowship.

Boyer, E.: Newsletter, May 1958.

Brain, R.: Newsletters, September 1965, 1971. Bible Christian Union.

Burroughs, J.: "Report on France." Conservative Baptist Foreign Mission Society, 1962.

Child Evangelism Fellowship.: France National Annual Reports, 1973-1975.

Christian Missions in Many Lands.: Missionary Calendar, n.d.

Cole, D.: "Report on Gospel Billposting." Report to Foreign Workers Conference, 1952.

Conservative Baptist Foreign Mission Society: Annual Reports, 1962-1979.

      .: France Executive Committee Minutes, August 22, 1968.

      .: "Paper on Strategy," n.d.

      .: SemiAnnual Report, July 1965.

.: "The Villa Concept." n.d.

Eastern Mennonite Board of Missions and Charities."
1961 Report.

.: 1969 Thionville Report.

.: Report by Orie Miller, n.d.

Ellul, J.: Lecture to Foreign Workers Conference,
1971.

European Bible Institute.: Board of Directors
Minutes, March 18, 1942; June 23, 1952.

Evangelical Alliance Mission.: Annual Reports,
1953-1980.

.: Field Conference Minutes, June 1959.

.: "Guide Plan for France." 1963.

Evans, R.: Paper read to conference of Greater Europe
Mission, October 10, 1966.

Foreign Workers Conference.: Summaries and notes,
1952-1975.

Fogel, F.: "Current Methods of Evangelism Used by
Pentecostals in French-speaking Europe." Report to
Foreign Workers Conference, 1964.

Gegner, P.: Newsletter, February 1, 1967. Unevangelized Fields Mission.

Geiger, W.: "History of the Friends of the AEEI."
TEAM, 1973.

Global Outreach.: "Miracle in Paris," n.d.

Gospel Missionary Union.: Annual Summaries,
1970-1979.

Greater Europe Mission.: Annual Reports, 1956-1980.

.: Board of Trustees Minutes,
January 27, 1968.

            .:   "Together," November 1964, December 1970.

Harris, T.: "Work with the Antillians in the Light of their Responsiveness." TEAM, 1973.

Jesberg, J.: Newsletters, 1952, December 1954, June 1955, November 1956. TEAM.

Jesberg, J.: "Report on Progress for Securing a Building Permit at Orly." TEAM, December 11, 1961.

Johnston, A.: "A History of the Housing Program." Mimeographed paper. TEAM, 1973.

Johnston, A.: Newsletters, August 1960, June 1963, 1970. TEAM.

            .:   "Roman Catholicism and Scripture." Advisory Committee Reports. TEAM, 1970.

Johnston, R.: Newsletters, October 1955, Spring 1971. TEAM.

Julien, T.: "Church Growth and Total Strategy." Lecture to Foreign Workers Conference, 1969.

Kalioudjoglou, T.: Newsletter, n.d.   Christian Missions in Many Lands.

Matthews, R.: Newsletters, July 1964, March 1965, December 1965. Conservative Baptist Foreign Mission Society.

Mennonite Board of Missions and Charities: Annual Reports, 1954, 1957, 1958, 1961, 1962, 1967.

Mennonite Central Committee: Annual Reports, 1946, 1947, 1950, 1958, 1959, 1961, 1969.

Merkh, D.: Report to Foreign Workers Conference, 1972.

Mitchell, J.: Nesletters, January 1968, July 1968, October 1968, May 1970.   Evangelical Baptist Missions.

Mortenson, V.: "Fusion, Partnership, Collaboration." Paper read at TEAM, Semi-annual Conference, 1973.

National Fellowship of Brethren Churches.: "Chateau de Saint-Albain," 1967.

National Fellowship of Brethren Churches.: 1972 Report.

Orr, D.: Newsletter, January 1962. Unevangelized Fields Missions.

Pocket Testament League.: Newsletter, 1970.

Renick, J.: Newsletter, 1972. National Fellowship of Brethren Churches.

Shank, D.: "Review of Political, Economic, Social, and Religious Developments in Europe." Paper read to Mennonite Conference, 1967.

Slavic Gospel Mission.: Undated brochures.

Umenhofer, N.: Newsletter, April 1969. Unevangelized Fields Mission.

Unevangelized Fields Mission.: "The Effect of Roman Catholicism on Protestant Missions in France." n.d.

          .: Assorted newsletters and reports, 1962-1978.

Webb, C.: Newsletter, 1947. Church of the Brethren.

Young, J.: "Survey of Evangelism in French-speaking Europe." Paper read to Foreign Workers Conference, 1970.

Letters

Abbett, C. (Baptist International Missions) to the author, January 30, 1973.

Albrecht, B. (Global Outreach) to the author, April 14, 1976.

Anderson, C. (Baptist Mid-Missions) to the author, February 1973.

Aseltine, J. (Evangelical Baptist Missions) to the author, August 14, 1976.

Barnes, D. (GEM) to the author, June 5, 1974.

Barnes, D. to Johnson, D. (TEAM), January 28, 1953.

Belloni, K. to the author, July 16, 1976.

Bezanson, N. (TEAM) to the author, March 16, 1974.

Bliss, K. (Society for Europe's Evangelization) to the author, January 2, 1973.

Bonnelle, A. (Worldwide European Fellowship) to the author, March 1973.

Bordreuil, D. (Christian and Missionary Alliance) to the author, August 2, 1973.

Burke, R. (Baptist Mid-Missions) to the author, March 1974.

Campbell, R. (GEM) to the author, April 145, 1974.

Dubois, J. to Johnston, A. (TEAM), May 23, 1966.

Egeland, P. (TEAM) to the author, February 13, 1973.

Enns, A. (Conservative Baptist Foreign Mission Society) to the author, August 8, 1973.

Escande, A. to Webb, C. (Church of the Brethren), February 15, 1947.

Evans, J. (GEM) to the author, March 8, 1974.

Fisher, J. (Faculté Théologie, Paris) to the author, April 26, 1974.

Gannon, L. (Global Outreach) to the author, March 10, 1976.

Geiger, W. (TEAM) to the author, July 1975.

Hall, M. (Churches of Christ) to the author, August 22, 1973; September 24, 1973.

Hopkins, D. (Global Outreach) to the author, June 30, 1976.

Huffman, R. (Baptist International Missions) to the author, March 1973.

Jesberg, J. to Mortenson, V. (TEAM), June 13, 1955;
January 3, 1957.

Johnson, P. (Christian Missions in Many Lands) to the
author, July 1973.

Johnston, A. to Johnson, D. (TEAM), January 6, 1955;
September 17, 1958; December 19, 1958; May 17, 1960.

Johnston, A. to Taylor, K. (TEAM), July 3, 1964.

Johnston, A. to Mortenson, V. (TEAM), November 17,
1962; December 5, 1964; May 22, 1963; December 18,
1963; March 10, 1964; April 8, 1964; April 16, 1964;
May 16, 1964; July 3, 1964; September 23, 1964;
August 8, 1969, August 18, 1969.

Johnston, R. to Johnson, D. (TEAM), February 1955.

Kalioudjoglou, T. (Christian Missions in Many Lands)
to the author, July 1973.

Larson, A. (Unevangelized Fields Mission) to the
author, May 23, 1974.

Lyons, N. to Board of Directors, Greater Europe
Mission, September 6, 1950; September 14, 1951;
September 26, 1951.

Miller, O. to Good, G. (Eastern Mennonite Board of
Missions and Charities), September 14, 1954.

Mortenson, V. to Jesberg, J. (TEAM), September 23,
1955.

Mortenson, V. to Lazaro, L. (TEAM), April 22, 1966.

Mumford, E. (Baptist World Missions), to the author,
June 1973.

Olsen, W. to Jacques, E. (Conservative Baptist Foreign
Mission Society), May 10, 1970.

Peterson, I. to Mortenson, V. (TEAM), November 10,
1969.

Phelps, H. (Bible Christian Union), to the author, May
1975.

Preuss, C. (Faculté Théologie, Montpellier) to the author, April 10, 1974.

Renick, J. (Campus Crusade for Christ) to the author, May 7, 1976.

Smalling, R. (Missionary and Soul-Winning Fellowship) to the author, January 1973.

Umenhofer, N. (Unevangelized Fields Mission) to the author, March 1973.

Vajko, R. (TEAM) to the author, June 1974; July 20, 1976.

Wedel, D. (Gospel Missionary Union) to the author, April 25, 1973.

Wheeler, M. (Global Outreach) to the author, April 20, 1976.

Winston, J. (Faculté Libre de Théologie Evangélique, Vaux-sur-Seine) to the author, August 10, 1976.

Interviews

Personally interviewed by the author:

Aseltine, J. (Evangelical Baptist Mission), June 27, 1973.

Atger, M. (Alliance des Eglises Evangéliques Indépendents), July 15, 1972.

Barnes, D. (GEM), June 14, 1973.

Baumeister, M. (Worldwide European Fellowship), May 30, 1972.

Beach, K. (TEAM), July 3, 1973.

Bell, W. (North Africa Mission), October 7, 1972.

Belloni, K. (Child Evangelism Fellowship), July 3, 1972.

Bernardo, J. (Unevangelized Fields Mission), June 23, 1973.

Bittner, M. (Conservative Baptist Foreign Mission Society), June 12, 1973.

Blocher, J., June 15, 1973.

Brugman, D. (GEM), February 2, 1973.

Bryant, H. (Unevangelized Fields Mission), June 23, 1973.

Copp, J. (TEAM), July 4, 1972.

Clark, G. (Billy Graham Evangelistic Association), July 2, 1972; June 15, 1973.

Dixon, D. (Conservative Baptist Foreign Mission Society), March 6, 1973.

Enns, A. (CBFMS), August 19, 1972.

Evans, M. (Operation Mobilization), June 16, 1973.

Evans, R. (GEM), July 20, 1972; March 6, 1973.

Feryance, D. (Baptist Mid-Missions), June 12, 1973.

Fisher, R. (UFM), June 22, 1973.

Fogel, F. (National Fellowship of Brethren Churches), February 1, 1973.

Gannon, L. (Bible Christian Union), June 19, 1973.

Geiger, W. (TEAM), June 11, 1973.

Good, G. (Eastern Mennonite Board of Missions and Charities), May 17, 1976.

Haas, J. (National Association of Free Will Baptists), June 18, 1973.

Heijermans, H. (Worldwide European Fellowship), December 15, 1972.

Hitt, R., December 15, 1972.

Hock, J. (Global Outreach), June 26, 1973.

Hopkins, D. (Bible Christian Union), June 23, 1973.

Horton, F. (Emmaus Institute), June 15, 1972.

Hoyle, R. (GEM), July 4, 1972; June 14, 1973.

Inman, B. (Baptist Mid-Missions),, August 21, 1972.

Jacques, E. (CBFMS), January 31, 1973.

Jesberg, J. (Pocket Testament League), December 14, 1972.

Johnston, A. (TEAM), July 19, 1972, June 13, 1973.

Johnston, R. (TEAM), July 15, 1972; June 21, 1973.

Julien, T. (National Fellowship of Brethren Churches), June 20, 1973.

Klein, G. (Christian and Missionary Alliance), January 17, 1972.

Knight, D. (Unevangelized Fields Mission), June 20, 1973.

Kornbau, R. (Global Outreach), June 26, 1973.

Larsen, A. (UFM), December 15, 1972.

Lazaro, L. (TEAM), June 30, 1972.

Lee, H. (Southern Baptist Convention), June 29, 1972.

Mathews, R. (CBFMS), June 20, 1972.

Merkh, D. (National Association of Free Will Baptists), June 19, 1973.

Miller, M. (Mennonite Board of Missions), June 16, 1973.

Mitchell, B. (Evangelical Baptist Mission), January 17, 1973.

Mumford, E. (Baptist World Missions), May 16, 1976.

Munn, R. (GEM), July 2, 1973.

Nesbitt, J. (UFM), July 18, 1972.

Olsen, W. (CBFMS), June 13, 1973.

Phelps, H. (Bible Christian Union), June 30, 1972.

Reeves, D. (Campus Crusade for Christ), June 22, 1973.

Rowley, M. (Bible Christian Union), June 26, 1973.

Rudy, J. (GEM), June 14, 1973.

Rumsey, W. (Worldwide European Fellowship), October 9, 1972.

Shaw, M. (Christian Missions in Many Lands), July 2, 1972.

Skuce, E. (UFM), June 21, 1973.

Stauffacher, J. (Baptist Mid-Missions), June 12, 1973.

Strock, L. (Baptist Mid-Missions), June 12, 1973.

Tabailloux, M. (Foyer Evangélique), June 28, 1973.

Troper, P. (Operation Mobilization), January 18, 1973.

Vajko, R. (TEAM), July 2, 1973.

Weiler, J. (Jeunesse pour Christ), June 28, 1973.

Wilkes, J. (Southern Baptist Convention), June 11, 1973.

Wilson, C. (TEAM), June 21, 1973.

Winchell, R. (TEAM), February 2, 1973.

Winston, J. (Faculté Libre de Théologie Evangelique, Vaux-sur-Seine), July 3, 1972; June 13, 1973.

Witmer, R. (Mennonite Board of Missions), June 14, 1973.

Wolgemuth, S. (Youth for Christ), February 3, 1973.

Other Sources

Copp, J. (TEAM). Personal notes.

Evans, R. (GEM). Personal notes.

Mitchell, B. (Evangelical Baptist Missions). Personal notes.

Questionnaire. Sent by author to over two hundred missionaries.

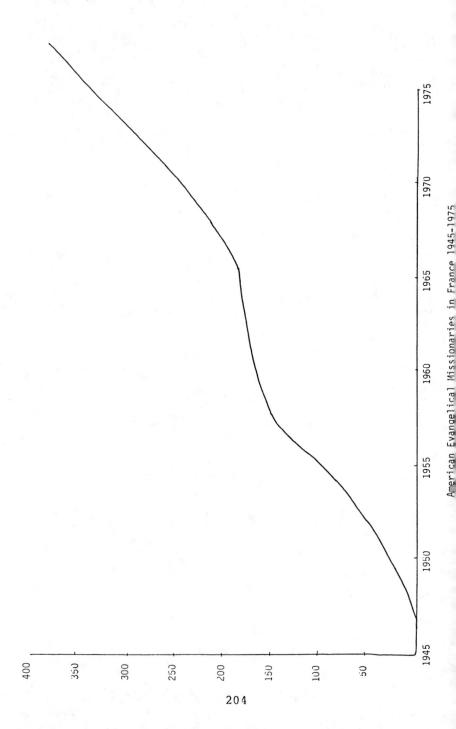

American Evangelical Missionaries in France 1945-1975

INDEX

Aerni, John and Betty 52
Alliance des Eglises Evangéliques Indépendantes 85,
     119, 122, 152, 153
Alpine Mission to France 91, 92, 115-118, 175
American Baptists 6
Assemblies of God 108, 111
Atger, Marc 153

Baptist International Mission 110
Baptist Mid-Missions 31, 32, 34, 46, 86
Baptist World Mission 110
Barnes, David 45, 52
Barnhouse, Donald 26
Bernardo, Jane 91
Bible Christian Union 6, 30, 86
Blocher, Jacques 24, 31, 44, 151, 153
Bonjour, Irene 35
Bryant, Henry 116
Burroughs, James and Beverly 107

Campus Crusade for Christ 112
Child Evangelism Fellowship 32
Clark, George 47
Collins, Hugh 108
Conservative Baptist Foreign Mission Society 106-109

Descheemaecker, Marc 153
Dixon, David 108

Ellul, Jacques 22
European Bible Institute 15, 33-36, 44-46, 52, 118,
     124-126, 163, 165
European Christian Union 6, 30
European Evangelistic Crusade 30, 47, 110
Evangelical Alliance Mission (TEAM) 45, 47, 50-54, 58,
     76, 79-85, 98, 118-125, 128, 152, 153, 163, 174
Evangelical Baptist Missions 110
Evans, Jeanette 33
Evans, Robert 1, 6, 12, 27, 28, 33-36, 44, 45, 52, 65,
     97, 98, 124-126, 128, 129, 174

Feryance, Daniel 31, 34
Fisher, Ronald 116
Fogle, Frederick 49, 87, 88

Godin, H. 21
Gospel Missionary Union 112, 175
Graham, Billy 28, 29, 45, 47, 74, 75
Greater Europe Mission 36, 45, 52, 58, 85, 86, 99,
    116, 125-129

Hancox, Jack 96
Hoyle Ronald 86

Inman, Bernice 31

Jesberg, John and Ethel 53
Jeunesse Ardente 84
Johnson, David 51
Johnson, Priscilla 6
Johnson, Torrey 27
Johnston, Arthur 50-53, 76, 79, 82, 83, 116, 120, 121,
    123, 152
Johnston, Muriel 51, 53
Johnston, Rodney 51-53, 82, 85
Julien, Thomas 89, 113-115

Kalioudjoglou, Trifon and Priscilla 50
Kapitaniuk, William 50

Latourette, Kenneth 22
Leonard, Emile 14

McGavran, Donald 105
Maclean, Sutherland 116
Marty, Martin 5, 22
McAll Mission 3
Mennonite Board of Missions and Charities 48, 90, 91,
    175
Mennonite Central Committee 6, 48, 90
Missionary Research Library 41
Mortenson, Vernon 79
Munn, Robert 35

National Association of Free Will Baptists 109
National Fellowship of Brethren Churches (Grace
    Brethren) 49, 50, 87, 89, 90, 112-114, 172
Navigators 30, 47
Neill, Stephan 14
Nesbitt, James 116, 117
North Africa Mission 111, 112

Operation Mobilization 30
Orr, Donald 91

Peterson, Ivan 84
Phelps, Harvey 6, 30
Plymouth Brethren 3, 6, 50
Pocket Testament League 30

Roher, David 47

Saillens, Reuben 26
Slanz Gospel Mission 50
Sommerville, Arthur 31
Southern Baptist Convention 92, 93, 175
Stephan, Raoul 14
Swarzentruber, Orley 49

Tabailloux, Marcel 24, 114

Unevangelized Fields Mission 92, 115-118

Vajko, Robert 119
Vaux-sur-Seine 96, 97, 151

Winston, John Jr. 97
Witmer, Robert 90
World Council of Churches 21
Worldwide European Fellowship 110

Youth for Christ 27-29, 33, 34
Youth With a Mission 30

DATE DUE

DEMCO 38-297